D0342319

PERFECTLY
MISERABLE

PERFECTLY MISERABLE

GUILT, GOD AND REAL ESTATE

IN A SMALL TOWN

SARAH PAYNE STUART

RIVERHEAD BOOKS

A MEMBER OF PENGUIN GROUP (USA)

NEW YORK

2014

RIVERHEAD BOOKS
Published by the Penguin Group
Penguin Group (USA) LLC
375 Hudson Street
New York, New York 10014

USA · Canada · UK · Ireland · Australia
New Zealand · India · South Africa · China

penguin.com
A Penguin Random House Company

Portions of this book appeared, in a somewhat different form, in *The New Yorker.*

Library of Congress Cataloging-in-Publication Data

Stuart, Sarah Payne.
Perfectly miserable : guilt, God and real estate in a small town / Sarah Payne Stuart.
p.   cm.
ISBN 978-1-59463-181-8
1. Stuart, Sarah Payne.   2. Authors, American—20th century—Biography.   3. Authors,
American—21st century—Biography.   I. Title.
PS3569.T826Z46   2014   2013048095
818'.5403—dc23
[B]

Printed in the United States of America
1   3   5   7   9   10   8   6   4   2

Book design by Gretchen Achilles

TO HUNTER, TEDDY, AND EMILY.

AND TO CHARLIE

The names and some distinguishing characteristics
of private individuals have been changed.

CHAPTER ONE

FLEEING MARMEE

IF YOU COME FROM NEW ENGLAND, the creeping certainty that you are a bad person is always with you. It wakes you with a start at four a.m. with the remembrance of a thank-you note forever unwritten. It asks you to please explain yourself when you pick up your dry cleaning on ONE DAY SPECIAL three weeks late. It darts out through the dental hygienist's reprimand that you are the captain of your own ship. Whoever and wherever you are, if you come from this

---

Concord, Massachusetts: a Protestant Disneyland.

stern mother of our country, a spark of your innate unworthiness is embedded in your soul.

But then, there are those brief, shining moments when you don't hate yourself. Joy is everywhere. We see it in the old houses and historic town centers that deepen our landscape with a past whose beauty surmounts its burdens; we see it in the endless meadowlands and fields and woods running wild under our careful conservation. Yes, we are sinners in the hands of an angry God; still, looking around us, we can't help but believe that someone up there might like us just a little bit more than He likes everyone else. We are like our Puritan forefathers who loathed themselves on the one hand, and thought they were above everyone else on the other. We love our Puritan ancestors, as most of our friends are sick of hearing—though sometimes we wish they'd left us a little more money.

New England can be as stingy with its welcome as it is stingy with its weather. But catch New England on a good day and there is a cozy uplift to the scene that takes the breath away. The sight of the hardy, high-spirited children, released from school on a perfect September afternoon to run through the antique towns, will draw even the most confirmed West Coaster to the window of a local realtor. And yet, it should never be forgotten: New England is an unforgiving place. Like the adored but disapproving mothers who populate it, it grips its children in the vise of its impossible expectations.

My hometown was the cradle of it all. Concord, Massachusetts, settled by Puritans in 1635, is "America's oldest continuously inhabited inland town," an official Facebook page will inform you, and the fact of this slightly qualified boast puts resolution in its residents' hearts today. Here, for the glory of God, rich English Puritans slept in mud bunkers penetrated by heavy rains, and sang psalms of thanksgiving, even as they cut their flat Indian bread into thinner and thinner slices. The rivers overflowed the pastures, the cattle died, the horses and sheep couldn't live on the land, and the wolves ate the pigs. But did the Puritans complain? No, they bottled it up, making "griping" a punishable offense.

Here, Patriot mothers stored gunpowder in their chambers and sent their sons to war so they could have taxation *with* representation. Here the great Emerson conceived a religion so lofty nobody has ever been able to explain it, yet lagged for fifteen years behind his wife in the antislavery cause. Here, for his whole life, Henry Thoreau lived, above it all perhaps, but still with his mother, and—despite his independent spirit—unable to live anywhere else.

Here also Nathaniel Hawthorne lived, next door to Louisa May Alcott and her pontificating parents: the useless Bronson, lounging on his front lawn with an apple, hoping to tempt someone (*anyone*) into conversation; the guilt-tripping "Marmee," overburdened and not keeping that fact to herself, slamming the door of Orchard House as she bustled in and out with moralistic platitudes and baskets of good deeds. Marmee who made her daughters grieve each selfish thought; Marmee who couldn't resist dragging a quiet moment down with a lecture; Marmee who reprimanded the rich, even as they gave to the poor, on why they didn't give more. Hawthorne avoided Mrs. Alcott at any cost, slipping through the woods behind his house seeking alternate routes to town; his wife, Sophia, had looked both ways before stepping out, fleeing at the sight of Marmee.

Yet it was Marmee, the most disapproving woman of all time, who inspired the most popular girls' book of all time, *Little Women*. And it was her daughter, Louisa May, who, though not perhaps the most profound writer of the revered "Concord Authors," was for me the most affecting. Not that I wouldn't have happily married the wise and handsome Emerson, at any age you'd care to pick (if only for his house); not that Hawthorne's Puritan guilt doesn't make me feel at home; not that Thoreau's quest to regain his childhood isn't mine. But it was Louisa who'd been a girl in Concord, scrabbling for money with three siblings and mental illness in the house; Louisa, whose wishful, saccharine version of life with Marmee was far more of a utopia to me than Thoreau's no-frills cabin in the woods.

Even now I see Marmee, dusty and patched, falling exhausted in her chair by the warm but shabby hearth, her "little women" scurrying to plump a cushion. This very day I cannot turn to the loving group around Marmee in the frontispiece of *Little Women* without suffering a pang of longing. Even when I know there was no servant Hannah in the kitchen, but Louisa herself, scrubbing and cooking, when she wasn't churning out "moral pap" for children— all to take care of Marmee. For what girl or woman among us does not long for a nod from Marmee, to be assured that she is not as bad as she knows herself to be?

To this day in Concord, Marmees still bound from the bushes: matrons of steel, born and bred to outlast the men who once found something to marry them for; no-nonsense women of indiscernible ages out walking their dogs, slickered and zippered against the most promising weather, huffing disapproval as they go. "Why are the young always fixing up their houses?" one cries out to a near-twin companion. "What this country needs is a good depression!" These were the matriarchs of my youth, a landscape of cherished but not always cherishing women—mending their swimsuits, buying gingerly at the A&P, holding up the bank line with their satchels of rolled pennies, attacking their lawn with broken bamboo rakes. Some I have loved and some I have not, but all, with the flattening of a smile, could conjure a mother's rejection, reducing me to a speck on the floor. I fled them at eighteen. I went to Cambridge, to California, to New York. Away, away, and finally happy and married and writing advertising copy on Madison Avenue, and living blissfully beyond our means in a New York suburb, and writing a novel at last, and paying too much for things and never wasting one paper towel when I could waste six. And then I had children. Suddenly I was homesick for a childhood I had invented as surely as Louisa Alcott had invented hers. Suddenly nothing would do but return to the cold heart of New England. Whether to defy the mothers of my youth, or become them, I did not know.

AND SO, pregnant with my third child, I decided to move back to my hometown. "So the kids can have swimming lessons at Walden Pond!" I explained breathlessly to my husband, Charlie. I was in my thirties at the time, still radiant with the delusions that brighten the threshold of middle age. I'd just sold my first novel, which I shyly conceded would probably become a best seller. I had become the mother of two charming, kneesocked little boys, who I knew would never play with toy guns or grow up to be mortified by their parents. The future, in the days one dared contemplate such a thing, beckoned.

Of course, growing up, I had hated swimming lessons at Walden Pond, almost as much as I had hated hearing about Henry David Thoreau. Lessons were always early in the morning, as all group swimming lessons seem destined to be, before the water or you were warm, and the groups were so large, and I so athletically doltish, I could never grasp how you were supposed to breathe during the crawl, and year after year I was the tallest, most knobby-kneed, in advanced beginners. But even this ignominy had become just one thread of a tapestried memory, with the early morning sun glinting over the momentarily urine-free water, as Janie McClintock and I climbed off the bus at the trailer park across the street and sauntered barefoot over the blacktop and down the steps to the grainy, old-Band-Aid-infested beach.

Janie McClintock and Tammy Ross and Rusty Ryerson and every other neighborhood friend I'd had clubs with, and clubs against, had long since vanished, moved away from New England, out West, or anyway, west, catapulted from this strong, crisp mother of our country into various melting-pot colleges, then into jobs with potential and fresh-faced first marriages. *The Concord Journal* began citing other children who'd made dean's list or police log (or both), and soon each neighborhood friend was lost track of, most of their parents also moving away from this breathtaking, impossibly beautiful town, as if trying to make a quick getaway before there was nothing left to brag about. For Concord demands perfect childhoods; follow even the most perfect child into later life and you will find, at best, disappointment and heartache.

Nothing could have been more psychologically unsound than moving back to my hometown—where my parents still lived—to raise my kids. Once, I had scorned my mother's housewife ways and rolled my eyes at the liberal, cocktail-party politics of her garden club crowd. But now the protected childhood I had managed to be so bitter about was to be gloriously re-created for my kids, with my own vast improvements, as my mother and father watched.

And yet, the truth is, I was never happier. We moved in July, and the sun coursed through the old house Charlie and I bought a quarter of a mile from the house I'd grown up in. My childhood home had bordered the railroad tracks, but this house was on the river. We had large delphiniums in the back and the boys ran in and out into the yard at will. With our new line of credit, we were no longer strapped for money. We'd been strapped ever since Charlie had quit his job in New York to start his own business so we could move to New England, but now we had extra cash. "Enough to send a kid through college!" we might have cried, we (the children of savers) with not one penny saved for retirement. But instead of saving one penny, we spent it like stolen money, breathless with greed. Like a roaring river, we poured cash on our modest farmhouse. We painted and wallpapered and added on a sunroom and an office and put up carved moldings, all in the space of six months, in a frenzy, lest cooler heads prevail. Excitedly, but anxiously, I flouted the penny-pinching standards of the town mothers on the one hand, and cravenly craved their acceptance on the other. My own mother, though worried that we were spending too much, seemed as thrilled as I was with our endless renovations. The old house shone with newness. And we shone too.

Euphoria pulsed through me. I wandered the Concord streets weepy with adoration for anything that had ever happened in my youth. The sight of the dentist's door, still with the same lettering, where I had averaged five cavities a visit, filled my heart to brimming. I gulped down sobs as I took out books from the library, where my red candy stain could still be found on its copy of *Little Men*, the drab, age-less librarian of my youth eyeing me, unmoved. I croaked brokenly for a loaf of bread as I came through the swinging doors of the Sally Ann bakery. I rented an office downtown in my former school, Emerson Junior High, recently reconstituted as a center for the arts, where the Concord ladies painted sunsets or sunrises. I walked down Main Street, past my childhood home, to my house, filled with sun and happy children.

I had barely graced a church since the day I didn't get revelation at my sixth-grade confirmation. But now I found myself attending the funerals of my parents' friends—some of whom I had only met a handful of times—as a venue for my flooding gratitude for being home again. During one funeral, my father sat quietly in the congregation, only to look up and see me, lurching up to the communion rail in a clinging black dress like a secret mistress, my eyes blinded with tears for a man I would not have recognized on the street. When the congregation rose to sing "Onward, Christian Soldiers," I collapsed into the seat with a yelp, so overcome was I with emotion.

I had returned, the prodigal daughter, to the perfect town, nearly perfect myself: a mother of three, well married, well housed, well careered. For even my semiautobiographical novel, which had produced months of daily migraines as I awaited its publication, had passed my mother's inspection. "It is a good book, and well written," she had informed me rather formally by letter, addressed to

Mrs. Charles Stuart, on stationery with *Mrs. William M. Payne* printed at the top. My book had been sanctioned by my mother—if only in our husbands' names.

I thanked the Lord, whoever He was, as I drove past the familiar old houses to the pristine town center, gleaming with historically correct colors. For whoever God was, clearly He resided here, where the white church steeples pierced the azure sky and the upright Concordians walked briskly to the ATM, knowing the money would always be there. I felt accepted—by the town, and by the God that had guided it, ever since the first Puritans had hacked their way through the wilderness, bleeding through their silk stockings—willing to risk freezing, starvation, and the loss of their scalps in order to pray all Sunday morning *and* all Sunday afternoon to their unforgiving God.

And it seemed that that unforgiving God was my God. Because what I felt those first glorious months back in Concord was forgiven: filled with the grace of God's—and my mother's—approval.

CHAPTER TWO

GOD AND MY MOTHER

ON THE BRIGHT SIDE of Protestant self-loathing is the industry it provokes. Louisa Alcott wrote a brutal fourteen hours a day, long after she had made more money than her family needed. Even the great picnicker, Henry Thoreau, could not justify the indulgence of living in nature unless he turned it into work. Despite his talk of indolence, Thoreau could not walk in the woods on a weekday morning, as my mother did with Mrs. Potter, simply to look at

---

Everyone in Concord was an artist, except my poor mother.
The Concord Art Association.

the fall leaves: he had to transform the experience into a book for posterity.

And yet, even for my mother a walk in the woods had a purpose—to take the fresh air on a Monday morning as befitted those fortunate enough to have been born into the Protestant Elect. One of the goals of the Concord matron of my mother's generation was to stand monument to the fact that, though *never* idle, she did not work for money—to prove, in my father's parlance, that she was a lady. And so, though my father's salary as a mattress salesman did not go far in supporting four children, my mother never considered taking a paying job, even after we had all left home. "What would I do?" she would query guiltily. "Work in a dress shop?" A feeling of accomplishment was important for a lady, as long as what you accomplished was ephemeral, like running a booth at the church fair or finishing a spring clean of a house. When I asked my mother what her friend, "the poetess," had published, my mother loftily answered, "She would *never* publish her poems, it would ruin them." My mother had tremendous drive, but much of the fervor of her Protestant ambition was channeled into the age-old question of whether to have peas or carrots for supper.

My parents had been through a war, my mother's nervous breakdown, four births, and five real estate transactions by the time they moved to Concord in 1957, and in

Concord they finally found themselves. In Concord, they fit in, as they had never fit in in Hamden, Connecticut, where everyone had gone to Yale; or Westchester County, New York, where the curtains matched the slipcovers. My parents were, in terms of their tribe, "well bred," as only a New Englander or a Southerner could be—meaning they were nice to everyone and especially nice to the cleaning lady. They knew how to serve a tennis ball and throw a fun, fuss-free party (with my father on Dixieland banjo, and an enormous sausage and rice casserole from *The I Hate to Cook Book* for soaking up the alcohol), and their humor was always at their own expense. My parents would have sooner died on the cross than discuss money with their friends, which worked out particularly well since they didn't have any money to discuss. Some of the old guard in Concord were rich and some weren't, but everyone was so frugal it was hard to tell the difference. So though my father did not rise a jot in his career selling mattresses, nor my mother progress in any of her artistic hobbies, in Concord they were somebody.

It had been a sad day when the Simmons Company moved my parents away from Concord in 1969 as my father neared sixty. Like lambs to the slaughterhouse, they dutifully returned to Westchester County to mark time in a very nice house in a very nice town where they knew no one and no one knew them. They scheduled their days around Weight Watchers Maintenance diets and the unsettling visits of adult children who weren't very adult, and trips to the vet with their blind and deaf mutt, Scout; they held on to their Concord Country Club membership and subscription to *The Concord Journal*. Then when my father reached early-retirement age, they sold their house at a loss and joyously returned to a ranch house in the wrong part of town. For nearly thirty years, my parents re-resided in Concord, as happy, really, as anyone could ever ask to be. No matter what new tortures their grown children devised for them or what tortures my mother devised for herself, they were in Concord, where their friends understood who they were.

To the outside eye, my mother's life was a life of leisure, absurdly fortunate, lived in her favorite town, filled with friends and worthwhile things to do—for, to be content, the New England matriarch must always be contributing to society, if only to the society of other matriarchs. Mrs. Bridge, the midwestern lady of Evan S. Connell's 1958 novel, might go shopping and return home bemused because there was nothing left to buy, but the Concord matron has no time for such idleness. No days of shopping and lazy lunches and afternoon manicures for these busy women who have never needed to work. Within months of their deathbeds, they can be seen standing, staunch or bent, outside their pretty houses at nine a.m., waiting to be picked up by another octogenarian millionaire in an inexpensive car on the way to a prison-outreach meeting. Their schedules do not lag even as their husbands drop by the wayside, but are packed with charities, clubs, paddle tennis matches, and artistic endeavors. Since the days of May Alcott, the ladies of Concord have been sketching and painting with the clear-sighted purpose of finishing the picture to put it in a show in order to sell it to one another. Almost every one of my mother's peers was an artist. Even the acultural Mrs. Rockwell, who wanted to put fig leafs on all the statues when she went to Italy, has in her dining room a large watercolor of a bare beach in winter, which is pretty damn good. My mother was an anomaly, with no drawing talent whatsoever, but this did not keep her from taking lessons. Fortunately, nowhere to be found is her charcoal sketch that bears no semblance of a tree. And all that remains of her years and years of silversmithing classes are some old unmatched globs of silver, a few with pins soldered onto the back; my father's cowboy belt buckle, which my mother had presented him with at age eighty-five, much to the chagrin of my dapper father, who wore it concealed by a pullover sweater; and a delicate hammered bracelet of silver flowers she'd made during her year and a half at the mental hospital in White Plains, New York. "I may not have been with you when you were a baby, but I was always thinking of you," she said when she gave it to me several years ago.

And yet, if my mother did not possess the craftsmanship of her Concord peers, she possessed something in her past that distinguished her from them: she had once, before she was married, stepped beyond the safety of her circle to compete in the real world. At eighteen, she had moved to New York determined to become a professional actress—no better than a prostitute in the eyes of her proper Bostonian grandfather—and nearly succeeded, studying for two years, then going the rounds with the Broadway producers. Her years of studying acting had lifted her into the sublime, but trying to sell herself had been a torture she hadn't been able to withstand for more than nine months. She had tried to beat the odds of her New England upbringing by going before the public, flouting the maxim that one may only appear in the newspapers three times— at one's birth, wedding, and death. Who knows what might have happened if she had persevered? She had true comic talent, though I saw it in full display only once, during a rehearsal of the Concord Players' production of *Cinderella*, in which she played the wicked stepmother. The night before the first public performance, she had gotten violently ill. Soon after, even the Concord amateur productions were relinquished, because the high she felt when she acted interfered with the person she felt she should be—a New England lady who kept herself in check. Or, as she put it, the acting took her away from my father.

Still, my mother had the perfect life in Concord, as she herself would have defined it, despite the fact she had been dealt depressive genes and a selfish mother, and her daily joys were weighted down by the fear of rejection that had colored her life since infancy. The year I moved back to Concord, my mother had just been made chairman of the ladies committee for The Cripple School, cofounded by her grandfather (and of course no longer called The Cripple School). But even this clear mark of approval had pierced her like a poisoned arrow, calling forth childhood fears of disapproval, shooting anxiety through her neck and back, and rattling the nerves of her feet, so that she hobbled about at The Cripple School meetings, crippled herself, passing the hors d'oeuvres.

FOR THOUGH my mother blithely attended the nonsectarian Unitarian church in Concord, the terrors of a Calvinist God were always with her. My mother believed that even having an evil thought meant you were evil; that if one wasn't good, then one must be bad—just as her Puritan ancestors had believed four hundred years before, except with a bit more confidence in which side of the divide they had landed. My mother's ancestors had been so sure of themselves, in fact, they'd taunted King James for a pass to the New World and then prayed incessantly on deck the stormy way over, ignoring the jeers of the *Mayflower* sailors. A few years later, another ancestor, Anne Hutchinson—a wealthy mother of fifteen—had been so Puritan even the Puritans couldn't stand her. After publicly refusing to answer to any authority but God, she'd promptly been banished from the Massachusetts colony by Governor John Winthrop, eventually landing herself in New York, where she and five of her children were slaughtered by Indians. Despite being warned by friendly neighbors of the coming attack, she'd remained defiantly (possibly psychotically) at home, positive that God would protect her. Today Anne Hutchinson is remembered as an early advocate for religious freedom and her name adorns a highway in Westchester County and the school one passes on the way to Lord & Taylor in Eastchester—but as a mother, perhaps, the five massacred children might have felt she left something to be desired.

The rest of my mother's family had stuck to Boston— the Puritans' "city on the hill," built for all the world to view—long after the world had stopped viewing. Believing in "family" as a whole, if not always on speaking terms with some of its members, they'd married within— producing double-cousins, manic depressives, and relent- less books about their genealogy that not even the family read. They made money and lost money; wished they were dead and yet held on for dear life. By my mother's mother's generation, the family's religious fervor had dwindled to a single, soporific, society-approved hour in church on Sundays (when they weren't at their country houses where they rested from God). "Nonbelieving New England Prot- estants," my mother's first cousin, the poet Robert Lowell, called them, and remembering my great-aunts and -uncles chatting away merrily at funerals, I see his point. But then, my rich relatives didn't really need to have faith in God any longer because, clearly, God had faith in them—just look at their houses.

A large house wasn't just permissible in the Protestant ethic, it was a sign of election. The Puritans believed you were either one of the chosen (the Elect) or one of the Damned, as predestined by God—and worldly success or failure was one way to tell which one you were. Peter Bulke- ley, Concord's extremely rich reverend founder, may have lived in underground bunkers for many months, but he did bring a carpenter from England with him to build him what I am sure was a *very* nice house. For New England

Protestants, appearances are everything: they must look like they have money (and therefore clearly belong to God's Elect), and yet they must seem to care nothing for it. At the root of the tangled New England neurosis is a deep respect for the money it loathes.

So the one luxury the old money permit themselves is a well-proportioned house in the right part of town, big enough to allow its owners to complain that they can't afford to live there. The bedroom floors are ice cold with a strip of thin, fraying carpet for one's feet to land upon from the tall, creaky, inherited bed (with its original mattress); the towels are balding with hanging threads; the ceilings are high, and the temperatures low in the winter and stifling in the summer; the food is plentiful, but plain and predictable, a rotation of meals handed down from generation to generation. But the houses—one gasps at the sight of their pillars and the breadths of their front halls.

My grandmother's generation was still rich enough that no one had to work for a living. But of course they *did* work for a living. My mother's grandfather, uncles, and cousins practiced as doctors until they dropped. A proper New Englander worked no matter how much money he had, just as his wife rose at seven-thirty to breakfast at eight, no matter how much leisure time stretched before her. For many years, I assumed that all doctors made fabulous salaries, remembering visits to imposing family compounds—the immaculate basement awash with cooks and servants, the cavernous upstairs with paneled libraries and long, glistening dining rooms. But as it turns out, my mother's mother's family had been living off the ever-diminishing fortune of an ancestor who was, according to someone or other in the family, "the first millionaire in New England." The dregs of this fortune, by the 1970s, provided its recipients with just enough annual cash for a year's tuition at Harvard, at about the time their children were no longer getting in (merit having so rudely entered the admission equation). Of course, the millionaire ancestor was a sketchy character, having made his money pirating British ships during the War of 1812. But never mind. Nothing is so persuasive of one's Elect status than financial success. When the family offered his portrait to Harvard, it was graciously accepted.

My mother's mother had grown up in an enormous house in Boston, winter weekending at a nearby farm and summering at a large, rambling Victorian compound in a fashionable Maine enclave. Though the live-in servants outnumbered their employers in my great-grandparents' establishments, somehow more help was constantly being brought in. Someone even came in to shampoo my teenage grandmother's hair—what a life!—and yet money and affection were studiously withheld from my grandmother early on, in the great Victorian fear of "spoiling" that seems to particularly afflict those who, having inherited their money, have been spoiled themselves. Even as a little girl, my grandmother had daily chores to do, and whenever she was "wicked," she'd been locked in a closet. Her parents, combining overindulgence and overpunishing, had followed the perfect recipe for producing a narcissist.

As a mother, my grandmother showered her own little girls with an erratic demonstrativeness, then dropped them cold for weeks at a time, in the care of constantly fleeing servants. She breast-fed my mother with a flourish against the prevailing upper-class custom, then abandoned her, aged six weeks, to spend months with her husband in the army. My mother had regular tantrums as a little girl, as my grandmother had, and my grandmother punished her in the same tried and terrible way she had been punished, dragging her "wicked" screaming toddler up to the attic and locking her in a closet for hours. My mother had few memories of her quiet, Bostonian father, who died of cancer when she was four. But she never forgot the time he crawled from his deathbed up the attic stairs to release her.

My mother, the eldest, and her nearest sister fought violently, hitting each other with hairbrushes. They were the devils, while the baby was my grandmother's salvation.

"My angel," my grandmother called my youngest aunt, who grew up to have a healing warmth and frequent manic breakdowns, chain-smoking herself to an early death. Once, my grandmother left her three girls under five alone in a hotel bathtub while she met a friend at the bar. Today, such behavior would have sent my grandmother to family court or worse. And yet my grandmother was not mean-spirited—she just could not see beyond her own over-powering needs. She felt the full range of emotions—when her daughters had breakdowns as adults, she wailed at their bedsides with guilt—it was just that her emotions were centered on herself. And, as is so often the case with the selfish mother, her children only loved her more.

My grandmother was distraught after her husband died, but she was still young, and though not beautiful, "she had *it*," my mother said. (A quality she maintained that she herself had lacked: "I was more beautiful than you," she told me when I was a teenager, "but you're much sexier.") After a year of weeping and drinking and relegating her children to servants, she fell wildly in love, not with any of the nice, cousinly Bostonians paying her court, but with the least child-friendly of the lot—a handsome Russian nobleman who had escaped the Bolsheviks with daring escapades and no money. My mother's new stepfather was decidedly *not-Boston*, exuding an assured, open sexuality seldom seen in my family's polite, confining circle. He was the successful-with-women kind of man who evinces genuine surprise when anyone declines his advances. "What she needs is a good roll in the hay," he once laughed about a less-than-compliant maiden aunt within hearing.

Things did not go well with the stepfather. He was the opposite of my mother's gentle father and insisted on his own way, dominating the dinner table down to the ultra-rich Russian food served by a Russian cook. He had affairs with secretaries, ballerinas, society matrons, and at least one pair of sisters. My grandmother remained enamored of him, dashing off for long romantic trips and allowing him full rein in the discipline of her daughters. My mother's nearest sister was openly fresh to him but it was my less demonstrative mother who hated their stepfather most of all. My mother had always been called the beauty, her next sister, the brain (who, advanced to my mother's grade, ex-celled in the same class, daily ingraining my mother's belief that she was stupid). By the time my mother was awkwardly turning thirteen, she was developing a body to go with a face that had been Liz Taylor–beautiful from birth. Her stepfather began caressing her arm and talked openly about the fine progress of my mother's "developing bosom." Life became intolerable for her.

When life becomes unbearable, it is usually from a

sense of guilt. My mother had been riddled with shameful curiosity about sex since she was five and her mother had taken her into bed after the death of her husband to rhapsodize about their ecstatic sex life. Night after night she'd waxed in too great detail, then warned my mother that she must never have sex outside of marriage—it was a terrible sin. My mother's one premarital affair, in her early twenties, had filled her with such guilt she divulged it to no one, not even my father. My father had gentlemanly held back the first three nights of their honeymoon in deference to my mother's supposed virginity. "I was dying for him," she told me, "but what could I do?" She had a point, for when, eight years and four children later, she finally blurted out the news a few days after my birth, my sweet but utterly conventional father had cried out, as he rushed down the hospital hallway, "My wife's a whore!" "I never want you to feel guilty about sex," my mother said to me years later, much to my surprise—and I never did.

My mother's stepfather was domineering and magnetic. Very likely it was the sexual feelings he continually provoked that horrified my mother. And when one night tempers flared and my thirteen-year-old mother ran out onto their city terrace and threatened to throw herself off, it was not so much because her stepfather had begun caressing her arm, but because a small, "evil" part of her had liked it.

CHAPTER THREE

A NEW BEGINNING

IN THE INDIAN SUMMER of my eleventh year—before my body began to complicate, before I smoldered my mother's bridal picture to ashes with a Tareyton cigarette, or engraved "I hate Mother" on my bedroom door—I called my mother "Marmee." It was my sticky tribute to the adored, if unfortunately named, matriarch of *Little Women*. Louisa May Alcott's supposedly autobiographical novel had intoxicated me in my last gasp before adolescence, its impossible

Dove Cottage, the Alcotts' first house in Concord, a charity rental from the family next door.

girlhood promises lifting me above the *Playboy* magazines and civil wars of my older brothers. I was sweetness, and I was light. I swept the kitchen floor wearing an apron and filled the afternoon air with brownies baking. My cousin, visiting from New York City, leaped into the fray, calling my mother "Aunt Marmee." We traveled trancelike from beds to sofas reading and rereading *Little Women*, Turkish Taffies pulling gently at our fillings. We dressed up as the March girls with nets in our hair and biked to Orchard House, the most revered Alcott domicile, to re-imagine the happy, innocent scenes of the pretty, prettily poor March girls. And though the real-life photographs of the Alcott girls might have shaken the belief system of the staunchest devotee, we soared above the hard evidence, past the five o'clock shadows of those mannish cheeks to the auburn curls and golden ringlets of Louisa May Alcott's imagination.

Though I had called my mother Marmee, she was not Marmee. She was neither the petting, pontificating mother of *Little Women*, nor the emotional tinderbox that was the nonfiction Marmee. The real Marmee had no way to stanch her bleeding wounds but with her daughters. She was desperate for the love she had never received from her own judgmental, cold, upper-class Bostonian father; the love deprived her by her own mother, dying young; the love she could never get from the husband she called "unkind, indifferent, improvident." Marmee (née Abigail May) had already lost a mother and several siblings when she had first fallen for the megalomaniac schoolmaster, Bronson Alcott. Teaching was a lowly profession in 1830s Connecticut, but when Bronson had chosen it, he had elevated it to the highest plane: through teaching, he modestly contended, he would do no less than save mankind. Some women like poetry from their suitors; Marmee preferred the reform of mankind through primary education. Marmee had pursued Bronson with an earnest exchange of jargon and zeal. Bronson had been touched by this woman burning up with his praises, and Marmee, mistaking the passion of Bronson's self-love for sexual passion, had poured all the heat of her loneliness upon him—only to be told after their engagement when Marmee's favorite sister died, *You should be thinking of me, not her.*

Marmee had had nowhere else to pour the passion of her unclaimed love but upon her daughters. She clung to them for support and made them cling back, united against the world. But my mother's neediness was never on display for her children; her goal was to be the opposite of her own mother who, though distant from her children whenever a man was on offer, was unbearably close when a man disappeared. My mother had found an affectionate husband for her confidences; if she had any other needs, her children would never know them. But Louisa grew up believing it was her duty to make her miserable mother happy, thwarting the chance for her own happiness. I may have longed for my mother to be Marmee growing up, but the fact is, my mother allowed her children to grow up in a way Marmee never did.

Marmee had lost a mother too young; my mother had barely had a mother. Both were deeply sensitive to perceived insult and prone to self-recrimination and hysteria. Surely my mother found her own mothering as emotionally fraught as Marmee had hers, but as a child I seldom saw it. My mother was the strict mother to be won over, regally tall and rigidly fair. Equal amounts were spent on each child; duties and allowances weighed to balance. If one child bought the comic books, the sibling who wanted to read them must rent them from their owner. Fairness is an obsessive trait in the Protestant gene pool, sometimes trumping merit and love. "Life isn't fair," my mother often informed us—but if life wasn't fair, it was not her fault.

One of my mother's stated goals had been to have eleven children. Her youngest was under two when she found herself pregnant with a fourth. She was absolutely sure that this time the baby would be the girl she'd always prayed for, but instead of being excited, she became very anxious.

She didn't gain the usual weight; she became anemic, thin, "very run down," everyone said. "I was afraid to have a daughter because of all the pain I knew she was going to find in the world," a friend once told me. Likewise, my mother's pregnancy had conjured up her own troubled girlhood—she hadn't known it, not consciously, but her body had.

Even her labor was different from the other labors she'd been through—easier, strangely easier. For the first three babies, she'd been put under general anesthesia, as was the custom. But even in the last throes of her fourth, my mother hadn't needed any painkiller; a wonderful happiness had descended, blurring the pain. She gave birth naturally to a baby girl, as she had predicted. It even looked like a girl, eight rounded pounds and curling eyelashes. My mother was delighted, nine months of worrying lifted; all was well, until the next day when she developed a blood clot, which required immediate surgery. Just as she was out of danger physically, she became horribly manic, conversing with the lightbulb as if it were Jesus, in the odd moments when my mother *herself* wasn't Jesus. Even during her mania, the one joy generally allotted the mentally ill, she was miserably flailing instead of ecstatically high.

The year and a half my mother was confined to a mental hospital in White Plains, New York, was not unusual in those days, when straitjackets, shock treatment, and occupational therapy were used in lieu of antipsychotic drugs. Her husband was allowed to visit once a week, her children, never. Some Saturdays my father was turned away because his wife couldn't handle the stress of seeing him. The second year, my mother was allowed home weekends, a more damaging situation than her total absence for both herself and her four children, who had to relive my mother's leaving again every Sunday afternoon, just after they had been so happy.

In the one picture extant of her weekend visits, my mother, dressed in pearls and Sunday best but looking as if her head is splitting, sits on the floor with her children, her eyes fixed on her baby daughter, too young to crawl but dressed to the nines in a starched white dress and matching bow, propped up between her sons playing a game. Being with her boys those terrible weekends had been difficult, my mother told me decades later, but being with me had been unbearable. The birth of a girl had been the trigger for her breakdown, she'd decided in therapy; she'd been terrified she would repeat her mother's mistakes. Finally, tense and skinny, but glittering with a sharpened beauty, she came home for good. And then came the system of chores for her children, mimicking her scheduled routine in the mental hospital, her path to sanity there and now at home.

I was not yet two when my mother returned to the family, but even at that young age I was deemed "undemonstrative." My mother said I perched rod-straight in her lap when she tried to cuddle me, giving rise to her defining theory that "Sally is hard-boiled." A hugger I wasn't, but a clinger I was, hanging on to my mother's legs as she walked, hiding my eyes if anyone else addressed me. Even as I drifted to sleep, I clung to the sight of my mother out my bedroom window, merrily drinking cocktails with my father and their friends in the backyard. "Happy hour," my parents and their friends called preprandial cocktails because a) it was the one time they were allowed to relax with impunity, and b) only the Protestant could drink so deeply and limit it to an hour. Even through the late 1960s—when my rebellious brothers, scorning alcohol for marijuana or Transcendental Meditation, mocked my parents for being hopelessly "bourgeois" with their two carefully measured gin and tonics—the cocktail hour remained entrenched, more sacrosanct than ever.

A less soothing early memory is the rumbling, grumbling bustle of my brothers doing chores before school. Billy (age nine) laying out the lardy strips of bacon in the cast-iron frying pan before making his own lunch; he and Johnny (age seven) making up Hunter and my bunk beds (Hunter, having taken me as a baby under his wing, had insisted to my mother we share a room); Hunter (age five) "collecting the trash" with a Tom Sawyerish panache every morning from each wastebasket—a busy-work daily chore that surely my mother invented.

My father was transferred to Boston when I was six, and my parents—crushed by a mortgage they regretted taking and not loath to leave Hamden, Connecticut— moved the family to Concord, a more quintessentially New England town. Here, as if in step with the Puritan heart-beat, family chores intensified. Now there was a seemingly endless raking of leaves ("Why rake them so often when they keep falling down!" the brothers moaned) and groans of "Whose turn is it?" to mow the crabgrassy lawn with a constantly breaking, constantly cursed electric mower; and weeding of the six-foot-square vegetable patch; and clean-ing the whole house altogether on Saturday mornings in an unmerry way. It was a system that ignited so many argu-ments among my brothers it's no wonder I have seldom seen them perform a domestic task since without reluctance.

Whereas I secretly delighted in cleaning the bathrooms every Saturday morning, breathing in the intoxicating smell of Ajax and rubbing the old porcelain sink to a shine.

It was joyous to see the house clean—the navy blue stair carpet, for a brief shining hour, dirtless and dog-hair-less, napped and renapped with fresh vacuum marks! It was like surveying the dining table set for Christmas, gleaming quietly before the storm. Often for fun, I would rearrange the furniture in my room and slather it with lemon oil and pull the shades down and turn on all the lights to make the room as cozy as the fictitious Marmee's hearth.

In Concord, I was given my own room, large and yellow. "It's not fair," the brothers cried, "that Sally gets the best room just because she's a girl!" But about this, my mother did not negotiate. Even though it meant that the eldest, Billy and Johnny, sworn rivals, had to share a room, leading to so many violent fights with objects crashing, that Billy was sent to an Episcopalian boarding school in Virginia, where he was subjected to the verbal abuse of the "rat system," modeled on the practices of English boarding schools. He wrote long, desperate letters begging to come home, which surely broke my mother's heart. Yet we never saw it. She rose above her own feelings and insisted that my brother stay at that school *for his own good*. "Cut the apron strings," my father had said, and then her family had always believed in adhering to "the original plan," even when the original plan was proved wrong.

With my parents cutting back, we'd moved from a storybook house on a storybook lane in Connecticut to a peeling, banged-up Victorian with a broken porch on screeching Main Street, where whizzing cars claimed neighborhood dogs on a regular basis, and freight trains shook the house as they ran behind the backyard. The new old house, to a six-year-old, was almost scary, a gloomy disappointment viewed for the first time, eerily empty in the shadows of a stark streetlight on a humid night. Victorians were considered dated and ugly in the late 1950s, and the Concord house was so much cheaper than the house in Connecticut, my parents could buy it without a mortgage. The pretty white house in Connecticut had been bought with a $15,000 bank loan in a wild moment of hope and consolation after my mother's institutionalization, followed by three years of remorse. My parents feared debt of any kind, and the shabbiness of the Concord house served as a kind of penance for their hubris in believing, back in the Connecticut days, that my father would be making a lot of money.

And yet, despite my parents' making do and my brothers' constant fighting, Concord was a new beginning. I remember being almost instantly happy that hot August when we moved into the house on Main Street, with its gaudy, giant-flowered wallpaper and single full bath, and I remember my brothers and my parents being almost instantly happy too. To the right, to the left, and across the street were families also with four children each. No one on Main Street sent their kids to camp in those days or had yet inherited houses on Cape Cod, and all the mothers were stay-at-homes, letting their kids run as freely and recklessly as their dogs through the neighborhood and into town, from morning to bedtime. The first day, as the movers were dripping humidly over furniture, a cadre of kids my approximate age appeared in my backyard. Hand in hand with the token boy was Janie McClintock, leader of the pack, shirtless and dirty, from adorable freckled Campbell Soup Girl face to her tiny bare toes, disappearing into her feet as in the leper scene from *Ben-Hur*. Janie, I was soon informed, only had to take a bath on Saturday nights. Janie's family came from somewhere in Canada and existed in a plane above appearance-conscious New Englanders. Her parents were cool and played classical music and didn't belong to the country club and never went to church. Once, Janie explained how she asked her father for her allowance at the beginning of the month and her mother for the same allowance at the end of the month, a statement that shocked me more by its admission than its fact.

Within a week, my mother had also found a best friend, Mrs. Potter, who lived on the other side of Main Street, which backed onto the river. Mrs. Potter was from a similar

New England family, except one richer and saner. Her husband had a better job than my father, and her kids were
more athletic and lighter-at-heart than we were. Mrs. Potter was confident enough to make little remarks about people that my mother would have thought herself a bad
person for even thinking. "Corky!" my mother would say,
shocked but rejoicing to find in her new friend's humor a
kind of unqualified acceptance she'd never known. With
the Potters my mother could slip the bounds and so could
we. We had a dollar limit at Howard Johnson's, but if Mrs.
Potter said, "Oh, what the hell, let's take the kids for sand-
wiches at the Ritz," off we drove to Boston to sit on bro-
cade chairs and eat BLTs with garnished toothpicks. "But
the Potters are allowed to!" my brothers cried out one day
against the strictly prohibited rolling of one's corncob on
the margarine stick, and forever after—or at least for my
own children and their cousins—the rolling was allowed.

By fourth grade, my shyness had subsided and I began
winning approval from my surrogate mothers then and to
come: from Miss Flora, and Miss Sheen, who was so strict
in the beginning, and Miss Burgess, who decided I was
smart. We all did well in school—it was something our parents demanded, though they'd been C students themselves.
(Or worse: a carefully preserved report card of my father's

from Williams College shows an F in economics.) Not, of course, that my parents supposedly cared about *grades* per se—they scorned other parents who gave cash rewards for As—it was the *attitude* behind the marks that counted, just as it was supposedly the *thought* that counted with gifts. Great disappointment was expressed toward one A minus, received because their son's teacher said he hadn't "made the effort." Like so many well-meaning parents who had not achieved their own worldly success, my parents could not help hoping for it from their children. And like most children, we wished to provide it. For a long time we did not fail them. Billy got academic accolades at boarding school, Hunter's B-plus average was supplemented by his tremendous popularity with girls, and I was cited in *The Concord Journal* for getting all As. But it was on Johnny that the family success rested.

Math and science were the fields of glory in the days of fighting the Russians, and in these fields Johnny had tested "genius." Genius, when acknowledged by others, translates to fame, and fame is almost as good a sign of being Elect as money. The limited fame my mother's family had achieved during the country's beginning had diminished by the Revolution; fleeing as Tories, they began the long reverse of the family motto from *Cut down, we flourish* into *Flourishing, we cut ourselves down.* The only family members renowned outside New England in the 1960s were my mother's second cousin, Cleveland Amory, whose amusing book about Boston society had caused his unamused family to flee their hometown, and her "difficult" first cousin, "Bobby" Lowell, who'd been considered "impossible," until he'd won the Pulitzer Prize.

Since kindergarten, I had bragged about my brother Johnny to an uncaring world, which included Johnny himself, who barely acknowledged my existence, shutting himself in his ultra-tidy room to study every afternoon into the night. His teachers were as competitive about their school as the rocket scientists about their country, and they urged upon their star pupil extra courses and math years ahead of his grade; he won so many different kinds of trophies his senior year, my parents had an enormous felt-lined cabinet constructed for them at great expense—to the horror of my brother who was too driven by guilt and loneliness to ever be conceited. By the time Johnny went off to Harvard, our family's reflected success eclipsed even the Potters'.

But at Harvard, there was no one to approve. Johnny was lost in the large lecture classes, where professors didn't even know his name. His high school girlfriend broke off their relationship, and he fell into a severe depression that lasted long into his sophomore year. The college health services prescribed him daily doses of amphetamines (used at the time as an antidepressant). The speed wore him down without lifting him up, and then he contracted pneumonia. Recovering, he felt wonderful, then too wonderful. He alerted his frightened roommates that he was Jesus, then panicked into hysteria, remembering the fate of that identity. His roommates took him to the college infirmary, which transferred him to a local mental hospital, where he was injected with Thorazine. My parents arrived, and Johnny was taken by ambulance to McLean's—the elegant, green-campused mental hospital in Belmont, Massachusetts, where so many of my mother's family members had "rested" since the mid–nineteenth century, along with Ralph Waldo Emerson's brothers and dozens of other prominent (but crazy) New Englanders.

MINE WAS NOT the first family drawn to Concord in the wake of mental illness.

Ralph Waldo Emerson, after settling in beautiful but sluggish Concord to start a family, had urged his crackpot friend, Bronson Alcott, to move there too. (Like so many of us when we first move to the suburbs and immediately regret it, Emerson wanted to drag everyone else there as well.) Forget teaching, Emerson told Bronson—you are here to produce great literature. But this was before Emerson had actually read anything Bronson had written. Soon he was fondly calling him "a man of no talent," if you can call that fond. Emerson had been totally taken in by Bronson, who moved seraphically in worn robes like the prophet he claimed to be. Emerson—with three manic-depressive brothers in and out of the bin—should have known better.

And so Louisa was about the same age as I when her family first moved to Concord, fleeing her father's latest disaster, and for her family too, Concord was a new beginning. Like us, the Alcotts had arrived in town with relief, recovering from the breakdown of a parent. Mob violence had been threatened in Boston after Bronson had published a record of his latest wackily innovative school, in which he'd compared himself to Jesus and quoted six-year-old Josiah Quincy discussing sex. The family was deeply in debt, moving into Dove Cottage, small and low, a charity rental from the neighbor next door.

One of the few happy memories of Louisa Alcott's sad life was of running as a girl in the woods around Concord's Nashawtuc Hill—where "Squaw Sachem" and her tribe swam and fished in the 1630s, before selling out to the Puritans at the bottom of the market; where Janie McClintock and I biked in the 1960s with our lime-flavored Pixy Stix; where teenagers today still bare their souls over cans of

Bud Light, and the leisured well-to-do walk their dogs, grateful to be themselves. And though as an adult Louisa escaped Concord whenever possible, returning only because her father could not stand to live anywhere else, still, she never forgot huckleberrying with Mr. Thoreau or the rustle of leaves in the sun-splattered forest when she first ran free in Concord.

But while my family had been able to present itself in town with the sheen of a normal family, the Alcotts were still shaking. As Marmee knew by now, Bronson was mad as a hatter, and had been since his teens, when his wild spending sprees had forced his impoverished family to sell part of their farm. Bronson was—I say this from deep experience in the field—a manic-depressive, with a touch less emphasis on the depressive. There is no greater charm than the devil-may-care confidence of a person moving into a manic state—I couldn't help but admire my brother's magnificence in the 1970s as he'd fired employees at Harvard and convinced the bank to issue him another MasterCard, though he had no money.

A young child's dream is for her parents to be just like the other parents. Louisa's do-gooder mother was a nonbelonger, resentful of the richer mothers who looked down on a woman whose husband was a profligate, seldom employed kook. Her father was sometimes ecstatic, sometimes weeping; sometimes entrancing, sometimes tedious; sometimes running at the mouth, sometimes vowed to silence; sometimes preternaturally calm in the midst of a disaster, and generally the cause of the disaster himself. But one thing Bronson never was, was just like the other parents.

The move to Concord had released my brothers and me into the freedoms of our Main Street neighborhood. We had run barefoot the summer days and nights, dodging cars, putting pennies on the train tracks, smoking cigarettes behind the barn. Likewise had the move to Concord released Louisa into fields and woods that seemed delivered by God.

The problem was that other god—Bronson, the god of her household as fashioned by her mother. Early on, Marmee had bought into Bronson's self-idolization with a young bereaved girl's idealism. So when Bronson proposed taking the family away on a mad scheme to found Utopia, Marmee sold her last valuable, packed up her girls, and followed her husband into the abyss.

So too had my parents made Johnny the god of our household—and when Johnny lost his bearings, the family followed.

CHAPTER FOUR

MOTHERHOOD

"YOU'RE ONLY AS HAPPY as your least happy child" is the best description of motherhood I have ever read.

I don't know what was worse for my mother: Johnny, crazy, committed to McLean Hospital; or Johnny, sane, coming home again and blaming my mother for everything.

The problem is, he sort of had a point, though there had been nothing my poor mother could have done about it.

My parents switched from Trinity to the more liberal Unitarian church, where everyone agreed fiercely with everyone about everything.

He had inherited his manic-depressive genes from her, and his breakdown was grounded in her breakdown—his girlfriend leaving him triggering the trauma of my mother's leaving when he was five, during that honeymoon period between sons and mothers.

While Johnny had ranted in a padded cell, my mother had waited in the ambulance that would take him to McLean's. "Don't crucify me!" Johnny had raved earlier, strapped to a gurney. But when he saw my mother in the ambulance, he had felt suddenly at peace; for a moment, the cold, gray world was bright with second chances. He was five again, and his mother was there. This time he could amend the behavior that he was sure as a five-year-old had caused my mother to go away. He promised my mother he would be a good boy, if she would just let him come home. How my mother stood it I do not know.

I do not know, because my mother never told me, or anyone else. I, like Marmee, would have blabbed my pain to the world; my mother kept it in. Whether her family had developed a companion gene to manic depression, allowing members to remain calm in the midst of craziness; or whether my mother's strong protective instinct toward her children trumped her own despair; or whether she despaired, but in private, I will never know. Growing up, I never saw her crying except when angry. Fighting with me as a teenager had sometimes pushed her into a short-lived hysteria, reminiscent of her daily childhood tantrums. But she never unloaded her sadness on her children, as her own mother had, and as Marmee had with her little girls. As a result, I never felt, as a child, that I had to make my mother happy. Next door, Link Linkin was always vacuuming the house while his mother, "unwell," lay for weeks at a time on her canopy bed; when Patty Best's mother had an affair, somehow it ended with all her children around her comforting her in her guilt. But I, as healthy children should, thought mostly of myself.

I was simply told that Johnny was in McLean's because he had had a breakdown. McLean's I took in stride—it was where Cousin Bobby went. As for Johnny breaking down— I'm sure my mother would have answered at least some of my questions, if I had asked them. But I was thirteen. I never asked what was wrong, or how my brother was feeling, or even if I could visit him. I was also told, almost in passing, that my mother had had a breakdown years earlier, but about this too I seemed to have no curiosity. I was too busy being an eighth grader, watching my nose morphing on a daily basis, and eating cake batter all weekend with Miriam Bent.

My parents seemed the same. My mother was still on schedule with her tri-part dinners at seven o'clock, with the

eternal syrupy canned peaches (or, with a dash of sponta-
neity, pear halves) for dessert. She was still always bustling
quietly near the kitchen coincidentally, or so it seemed,
when I arrived home from school to ignore her, as I ate my
cinnamon toast over *Lord of the Flies* or Salinger's *Nine
Stories*, or whatever else I was reading and appreciating for
the wrong reasons. It was a major point with my mother to
be nearby when we arrived home, and one that I held
fast to later in my own teenager parenthood. "I know you
hate me," she said to my brother Hunter once in the thick
of his rebellion, "but I also know you love me being in the
next room."

But of course my parents were not the same. My mother
had no favorites—we all yearned to be the favorite child,
but on this my mother was impervious. But my father had
been jealous of his wife's closeness to his first son—born
when he was away fighting in World War II and named
Bill after him—and had favored his second. When he got
the news that Johnny's Harvard roommates had taken him
raving to the infirmary, he'd flashed back to my mother's
breakdown fifteen years earlier. My father had a naturally
Zen-like constitution that allowed him to enjoy life in the
midst of tragedy, and a self-deprecating charm that allowed
him to get away with it, but I knew he was rattled. The
whistling through his teeth that had once heralded his

every approach was seldom heard. My parents drove the fifteen minutes to McLean's on a regular basis, I learned later, to listen to the psychiatrists carefully explain the myriad ways they'd caused their son's breakdown. It was the era in psychiatry where the child was exalted and parents, rather than genetics, were blamed, and my mother's guilt must have been extreme. It never occurred to me to notice.

Then the fall of my ninth-grade year, Johnny started coming home on his motorcycle for the hot midday dinners that bisected our Sundays between the boredom of church and the guilt of undone homework. He was out of McLean's now, editing math books to pay the rent on a dingy apartment in Cambridge so heaped with junk you were winded by the time you reached the dubious shore of the broken-down couch. Once shorn and immaculate, he dressed like the jazz musician he had become, in dirty black jeans and purple T-shirts and long bumbling hair. When he was coming for dinner, I would lemon-oil the dining room table and set it with all the things we never used from the old corner cabinet, down to silver baskets for salt. Then, "I didn't ask to be born!" Johnny would remind my parents as he ate, flaunting his bad table manners, as well as the details of his sex life, equal Protestant sins. After dinner, Johnny followed my mother as she grimly tidied up the house, playing his sax and singing Bob Dylan's "The Times

They Are A-Changin'." My father would reprimand him, very upset, but my mother took it with Puritan fortitude, as if it were her earned punishment, her mouth stretched in strained forbearance.

My brother Hunter, a senior in high school, had metamorphosed too—from a popular madras-clad prep, listening to The Kingston Trio, to a rebel without a cause, with a Bob Dylan snarl of hair and the Tom Rush–inspired blue workshirts and tan corduroys that signaled you were cool. But I held on to my niceness. Just as I had openly played dolls too late in defiance of my brothers' mockery, I still wore the sex-numbing shirtwaist flower-print dresses they derided, with matching cardigans and tan nylon stockings held up by a monstrous Maidenform girdle I didn't need. Marmee would have been proud. To "excite . . . admiration," Marmee confides to her teenage daughters in *Little Women*, with perhaps the worst advice ever imparted on how to get a man: be "modest as well as pretty."

As I approached tenth grade, my mother offered to send me to boarding school, paid for by a proper but uncharacteristically generous Boston aunt. I picked a conventional all-girls school with nice dorm rooms. It was my last-ditch hope—doomed from day one—that I could be a flirty, happy girl, like Becky Borden, the perfect girl a grade ahead of me, with her flashing smile and tiny gold hoop earrings. Horribly homesick, I viewed the bright, pretty girls as if through impenetrable glass and crawled through the enchanting fall days with a lump of despair clogging my throat. For six weeks my parents insisted I stick it out. But things had changed since Billy had been forced to stay at boarding school—after Johnny's breakdown it was hard for my mother not to doubt her parenting instincts. The experts were supreme now, and just as the tuition became nonrefundable, the school sent me to a shrink in Boston, who informed my mother that I should come home. She could not protect me from my miserable brothers, he said, and that I wanted to be home to protect them. I glowed with joy, so very happy to be going home.

Home to Main Street I came, but not before my brother Hunter returned home too, within a week of leaving for college. Having the luck (the bad luck) to befriend a pharmacist's son, he had compressed a lifetime of drugs into five days and arrived home dazed. My father wanted to force him to get a job, but my mother, with three failures now charged to her account, deferred to the experts, and Hunter was sent as a day patient to McLean's. Ginger ale, his favored drink for the pot-soothing reasons my mother did not know, was ordered by the case. My allowance was increased. Money, once so guarded in the family, was released as solace, at my mother's insistence—as if in rebellion to the strict creed of her New England family, whose generosity seemed limited to manic-depressive genes.

As my mother tried to understand us, Hunter and I, the great disappointments, united against her. In the morning, Hunter dropped me off at high school on his way to the mental hospital's teen program, sanctimoniously explaining, in the car my parents paid for, how, like the equally sanctimonious Thoreau (who also lived with his parents and had no responsibilities—not that this was Hunter's point), he didn't *need* money. In the evenings Hunter taught me how to be depressed by damply nauseating myself with filterless cigarettes while listening to "Sad-Eyed Lady of the Lowlands" under his enormous headphones. On Saturdays, while other girls cheered the high school teams, I cheered the McLean's basketball team in their curious matches against any high school team that would agree to play them.

Every night, after my parents were in bed, Hunter toked up in the playroom in front of *The Tonight Show* with Johnny Carson (his one true friend), communing by phone with the other Johnny in his Cambridge apartment. My mother knew that Hunter didn't smoke pot in the house because it was her stated, if incorrect, belief that her children would never lie to her. When we were little, we had often been told we were bad. But after we actually became "bad" as teenagers, my mother swerved to a firmly hopeful view, defending us against our detractors. Many of my parents' friends and relatives were brutal, at least until their own children began to outdo us in rebellion. But even at our lowest ebb my mother would say, "Well, at least no one can say my children are boring."

Hunter had carried me everywhere like a lovey when I was a baby and my mother was in the hospital; now he was my guru in rebellion. On the weekends Hunter and I chain-smoked in Johnny's Cambridge apartment, while Johnny walked the perimeter of his disheveled living room, blaming my mother for everything and saying how miserable he was. Johnny had never deigned to speak to me in the glory days before his breakdown, but now I was his sacred disciple, puffing away sympathetically in my brother-approved Indian-print mini shifts and globbed mascara. Johnny, who'd needed a mother to save him at age five, now looked for a girlfriend to save him from the loneliness he could never dispel. He would talk for hours about a girl he'd seen on the street or at a sandwich shop, who in the wisdom of her smile, possibly pointed in my brother's direction, seemed to understand the universal truths. I prayed I could make Johnny happy as my mother could not.

Somehow it was my mother who was always the center of our disdain. My mother whom I aped doing the jerk or the twist at a jazz party, churning up and down like a corkscrew with gritted teeth; my mother, whom we laughed at, manufacturing chores for us that would have been easier for her to do herself; my mother, who, we laughed, stupidly "trusted" me with my pot-smoking brothers at the house when she and my father went away for a weekend. Though my parents were such a united front we called them "the parents," my father had always looked like a sad little boy when he couldn't brag about one of his children, and so we protected him, blaming my mother for nagging him into supporting her strictures. What we were really, and un- fairly, blaming my mother for, was for leaving us after I was born, but, of course, none of us knew that, least of all my mother. She was neither *Mummy* nor *Marmee*, but *Mother* now—I put into that single word all the disgust I could muster. My father was still *Daddy*, and for Daddy—I said whenever I could work it in when my mother could hear— I would gladly give my life.

But for my mother I had not a civil word, slamming my bedroom door in her face after I had goaded her into losing her temper. Then, when my father would arrive home from work, out from my room I would burst, trouncing loudly down to give him a big hug. Dutifully my father would listen to my mother's reports of my various sins, and dutifully he would come to my room to scold me, but scold me he never could because I was his perfect little girl. My mother addressed even my vacillating weight as if it were a moral issue, but in my father's eyes I was a beauty queen at any poundage. He beamed at me as if I were Venus on the shell, as I stamped into the bathroom every morning, cranky and greasy-faced, with hair in popping-off curlers. It was my mother who, worried about her own unworthiness, worried about her children's. But my father didn't worry about whether he was worthy or not, and I didn't worry about gaining his approval, because I had always had it.

Around this time, my mother and father found a new god in Eugene McCarthy and switched from the mostly Republican Trinity church to the Democratic Unitarian Church, once the Puritan Reverend Peter Bulkeley's First Parish. Her own mother—combining an anarchic snobbish disdain for educating women with an inveterate cheapness—had not allowed any of her girls to go to college. As a result, my mother's mind had no training, and, truth be told, it didn't have an intellectual bent. But in the 1970s, becoming an intellectual was her keenest desire. She read whatever liberal writers were in the ascendancy and quoted them back to us with a finger in the air. "Mother has had *The First Circle* by her bedside for a year," I told my brothers within my mother's earshot, "with a little marker in the exact same place." Undaunted, my mother continued in her quest, seeking even to evoke "interesting conversations" with her derisive children. She informed us sagely that we were all products of "an affluent society," and listened to Eric Sevareid on the *CBS Evening News* with religious awe, and posted underlined newspaper columns on the refrigerator that nobody read. Once, when she made another of her philosophical remarks about "life" at Sunday dinner, I, who had barely touched my mother in years, reached dramatically across the table to grasp her hand, saying, as if blinded by her brilliance, "Thank you, Mother, I am now a new person." It was so nasty, even the brothers didn't want to laugh, but they did.

I thought for many years that I had been competing with my mother for my brothers' love. But really, of course, it was my mother's love I feared one day might be withdrawn. When we fought, I told my mother I hated her. She told me I was evil, when she was out of control. When in control: "I know you love me, else you wouldn't hate me so much." She was correct, of course, though it would take me many decades to realize it. Aged fifteen, sixteen, and seventeen, I mocked her stupid bright clothes and large plastic earrings; her stupid adherence to McCarthy when Robert Kennedy entered the race, even when she admitted McCarthy couldn't win; her cocktail party philosophizing.

"Being liberal is just a status symbol," I said witheringly. Nothing could have been crueler to my mother than to deride her brainpower. I hated myself, but I couldn't stop.

And then my mother got breast cancer and had a radical mastectomy. They hadn't thought it was cancer when she was going in for the operation, and then she'd woken up without her breast. "Your beautiful mother!" my father had cried when he came home from the hospital. The next day my brother Hunter went out to find a job. And I, feeling subconsciously that I had caused the cancer with my invective, never again told my mother a true thing.

CHAPTER FIVE

MARRIAGE AND MOTHERHOOD

JOHNNY HAD TWO full-scale psychotic attacks my freshman and sophomore years at college. Both times he had been going back to Harvard with me to complete his degree. Both times I tried to save him, in between ironing my hair and not going to classes because I was too busy smoking cigarettes and being in love with boys who didn't love me.

I told my mother—nothing. This is hard to grasp now

The Polaroid snapshot I carried with me everywhere,
gazing at it as if at a movie-star boyfriend.

when I, like many mothers of my generation, am sometimes updated on my college-age daughter's emotions on an hourly basis. ("I feel great now I've had breakfast," texts my twenty-year-old daughter Emily from England, "*though I did feel a tiny bit homesick when I first woke up.*")

But in the end, my mother succeeded where I had failed. She moved Johnny nearer her to a very nice state hospital in New York, and Johnny got well—becoming the only one of us ever to achieve fame, recording with Bonnie Raitt and soloing with Phoebe Snow on *Johnny Carson*, the show that had once been Hunter's and his shared solace—never breaking down again.

I manufactured my own misery the next few years, lost without Johnny's unhappiness to block my own. I tried a few times to enlist my mother's sympathy, but it was too late. My mother had a great capacity for empathy—it was to my mother my friends in high school had gone when they were in trouble—but she had been too full up with my brother's problems for my much lesser ones.

Instead, she sent me to the experts so I wouldn't "keep it all in" as she had before her breakdown. I saw the very serious Dr. Golden twice a week my junior and senior years, at crippling expense to my parents. But the day I graduated from college, the funding stopped along with all other parental funding: my mother believed firmly that her children needed to support themselves completely post-college (for our own good). "I pray every night that you do not go to graduate school," my mother said.

The shrink, on the other hand, was, not too surprisingly, totally opposed to my stopping therapy. He suggested I bring my parents to my last session, which I did, weakly joking over the phone that it would be kind of a shrink graduation ceremony to ease any fears that feelings might be discussed. We managed to achieve quite the festive air in the waiting room before the session, only to be greeted by a dour Dr. Golden. I had talked only of my mother in therapy, so I was surprised when he went immediately after my father, asking why he couldn't believe his daughter was unhappy. My poor mystified father, who could only look at his "attractive" daughter graduating from Harvard with all of life ahead of her, and think, *What in the world can be the matter?* My father shook his head and said to my shrink, "I don't care if Sally writes another sentence, as long as she gets married."

And the thing is, I agreed with him.

As a parent, my father was the opposite of Bronson Alcott. He was always rational. He looked up to his wife and children, not down. "Beats me how I got such smart children," he would breathe anew when each report card was presented. As opposed to Bronson, who plunged his family into stupefying debt and then declared himself above money, my father always supported his family financially and never risked changing jobs, no matter how much he hated them. Before my mother's breakdown, my father had hoped to rise in his company and often traveled during the week. But afterward, he settled into being a mattress sales-man, coming home every night at six. I told my friends my father was a "sales manager," just as I told them our mutt was "a mixed breed," but if my father was embarrassed by his job status, I never saw it. He was my security, and my constant, often sole, admirer.

No wonder Louisa Alcott never married. What was to like about marriage? She saw her mother enslaved to a man who saw only her faults. To attract men, women need to feel themselves attractive. Bronson had taught Louisa she was almost repellent, in both looks and temperament. My father taught me to feel attractive by thinking me irresist-ible to all others, through fat and thin. Louisa's father had taught her by example that men were not to be trusted. From the cradle, I had learned the opposite.

As a result, I married young, without having the least idea who I—or Charlie (in that terrible short orangey-leather jacket)—was.

———

I CAN BARELY REMEMBER a time when I wasn't looking for a husband. My first candidate was so young we couldn't pronounce each other's names. In elementary school, I quietly engaged myself to a new unsuspecting boy every fall. My junior year in high school, I suddenly became a joy to have in class, so I could get into Harvard, which had a ratio of four to one. After graduating, I took a low-level secretarial job because it was at the liberal public television station in Boston where all the guys were my type, meaning they were skinny and looked depressed. (My tastes had been refined at the McLean basketball games.) That year I kept a variable list of five guys I could marry. Charlie (the opposite of depressed) was my safety. To keep a list of five going, you sometimes had to go off-type.

And, the truth is—though this is wrong on too many levels to name—marrying Charlie did solve my life. It wrecked it too, for a couple of years—but you can't have everything.

Certainly it solved my life with my mother, at least temporarily. For nothing ever made my parents happier than my marrying Charlie: in one fell swoop, I was off their list of worries forever—no more extra car insurance, or birthday dinners to arrange, or *Guess who?* Valentines to send. Plus, Charlie not only came from Princeton, New Jersey, and had been captain of the hockey team at Dartmouth College, he had an actual job. This was the end of the 1970s. One of my brothers had recently returned from a meditation retreat where, for $2,000, he had learned to shrink to the size of a tiny little dot, for what purpose we still do not know.

My mother was so invested in Charlie as my salvation that when Charlie suddenly walked out on me after a year and a half of marriage, my mother ended up taking his side. First, biological instinct kicked in, and she rallied to her abandoned daughter, even admitting it would have been so much easier to handle if Charlie had just died. For a brief moment, I was a heroine in my misery, especially since I did not come home to live, like the Fosters' daughter who, two months after her glorious wedding, was back in Concord, jogging down Main Street in her trousseau track suit. But when, several months after the separation, I phoned my mother to announce that I would be seeking a divorce in order to get on valiantly with my life, the news was greeted not by applause for my Protestant fortitude, but by silence. I arrived home for a weekend visit to find all my wedding pictures, once so discreetly whisked away, now prominently redisplayed. "He's just not well," my mother said—employing the New England euphemism for someone mentally ill (the last thing Charlie was), as the only explanation for why anyone would leave her daughter.

Long after Charlie returned and we had three kids, my mother would still murmur to me worriedly, "You never talk about 'it,' do you?" And when I looked puzzled, she would say in hushed tone, "You know, the thing with Charlie." I assured her I never ever did, though, in actuality the subject of our one-year separation had happened to crop up casually in conversation on a daily basis for the past decade. At get-togethers with old friends, Charlie would clock how many minutes would elapse before I would say, "Of course, when Charlie left me . . ." and be off and running, relating embarrassing stories with gay abandon. Our children were barely able to grasp the fundamentals of *Pat the Bunny* before I breezily informed them, "Your father and I broke up years ago, so that's over and done with, you needn't worry."

Marriage won me my mother's approval, and when I first got pregnant, her happiness was complete. "Little mother!" she gushed, a little stickily, but I took what I could get. Why my mother was so eager for me to have kids when her own kids had been so difficult, I didn't think to question.

Charlie and I were living outside New York at the time, in a crumbling white elephant of a Victorian house, the first sight of which had caused my parents to cry in distress at the amount of work needing to be done to it. Unlike us—and unlike the Alcotts, Emersons, and Hawthornes for that matter, who were always pouring into their houses money they didn't have—my parents and their generation had never considered tearing down walls or building on new ones, accepting their structures as their fate, like pre-destined Puritans. Or, as they liked to refer to themselves thrillingly, like *children of the Depression.* For my father, with rich friends and no money, the Great Depression had been a great equalizer. For my mother, at drama school in New York City living on $2,000 a year from a tiny trust, it had been a kind of exhilaration to be "poor," a test from God to show how cheerfully she could eat spinach from the Automat for dinner. (Fake poverty has an allure like no other for those who live on disappointing trust funds.) Having any mortgage at all sent a shiver down my parents' spines, whereas Charlie and I had taken the largest mort-gage we could qualify for to buy a house so big we couldn't afford to heat it.

To me, the frigid Victorian was heaven, filled with cozy possibilities, even as its plaster ceilings fell in large chunks onto the beat-up floors. I carried a creased Polaroid photo of the house in my wallet and mooned over it, as if at a movie-star boyfriend. The house was our joy and avoca-tion. Every weekend we spackled and sanded and painted and wallpapered, collapsing at eight on a Sunday evening to survey the progress of our unoccupied rooms. We almost had to have kids, to justify the house.

I had never even babysat, and I had never imagined myself as a mother—it was too close to my mother's identity. By the time I was thirty, I had so defined myself as being the opposite of my mother that my shrink in New York said, "Well, you *are* both women so there are bound to be *some* similarities." This was after I had announced that Charlie and I were thinking of having children, hoping the shrink would say, "No, no, you are *too* young!" Or "Wait until the feeling passes!" Or, even better, "You're not the mother type!" She did not.

Natural childbirth was the moral high ground in the 1980s. My generation was fond of moral high ground: as teens we'd taken illegal drugs to prove something terribly important to our conventional parents (what it was is unclear). As prospective mothers we were now refusing legal drugs to (once again) prove something terribly important to our mothers, who had been put under general anesthesia to deliver their children and had clearly missed so much. I did not miss so much.

My first child, Hunter—named for the brother who had saved me as a baby—was delivered in the kind of shocked agony that must have originally given the Puritans the concept of "born in sin." Like most expectant parents, Charlie and I had not heeded the warning signals. Lulled by the baby powder tummy-rubbing of Lamaze class, Charlie had murmured one evening, "You know, this just might hurt me more than it hurts you." We had smiled inwardly at the shell-shocked couple crawling back to class to report on the horrors of the real-life experience, thinking, *Just who is being the baby here?* We'd arrived aglow at the hospital with our well-stocked goody bag. Then I'd been induced, going from nothing to two-minute contractions thirty seconds apart.

But, as it turned out, having children was the making of me—despite a little flurry of panic the day I returned from the hospital with Hunter and found none of the fancy baby books included instructions on how on earth to change a diaper (*I guess*, I finally figured out, *you just kind of wipe and put on a new one!*). Like my mother, I found myself looking for rules and finding strength in routine. Bedtimes, naptimes, storytimes, mealtimes were adhered to as if life or death propositions. Up we would get in the middle of a party or a meal at a restaurant if the clock was nearing the witching hour of the three o'clock nap. Starting at six months, Hunter was fed the same meal three designated times a day until he turned one, because I had once read something or other in a magazine about first solids. I carefully reported to the doctor: "I feed Hunter peaches and oatmeal at ten a.m.; then, at three p.m., I feed him peaches and oatmeal; then at eight p.m., I feed him—peaches and oatmeal!" "That's fine, Mrs. Stuart," said the nice doctor, "though some mothers find it more convenient to feed their children at mealtime."

It had never occurred to me before I had Hunter that I might possess maternal instincts or capabilities. I'd always been tongue-tied around little children and, like a Jane Austen novel, had never progressed beyond the end point of marriage in my life plans. Charlie had asked when he proposed—if you can call "I don't know, maybe we should talk someday about getting married or something" a proposal ("Yes!" I'd answered)—whether I'd consider having children. I was so thrilled that I hadn't killed Hunter after five months, that I had another baby nine months later.

All the fears I had about becoming a mother that I had inflicted on my first child vanished with my next. I was so relaxed during my second labor I experienced no pain, though I still requested the drug—just for fun. Hunter had been induced ten days late amidst his mother's curses, but Teddy breezed into the world three days early, spooned out of his blissfully drugged-out mother (even the umbilical cord about his neck at the last moment had not seemed to worry me) as convivially as a delivery from the stork. Teddy himself was so relaxed, he slept through his first three days, waking to find his brother had brought him every shoe out of his father's closet, as if to say, *You try filling these.*

I had nursed Hunter without distraction, with the concentration of a deckhand suddenly promoted to captain of a nuclear submarine. Straight into poor Hunter's eyes my own eyes had bored with arrows of love—eight nursing hours a day, at regular intervals. During the midnight feeding, Hunter would peer wide-eyed at my large prescription sunglasses while I sang "Five Little Ducks," moving myself to tears at the finale when the baby ducks at last (!) return to their mother—with the result that one of Hunter's early sentences was "Mommy, don't sing." Teddy, on the other hand, was nursed whenever he made a peep, lying with me in my white eiderdowned bed, as I slept through *Dynasty.*

Having kids even solved my writer's block. "I can't write because I'm not depressed enough!" I had driven Charlie wild with that proclamation since the day I'd met him. But after giving birth to Hunter and Teddy, I suddenly wrote a novel because it was so much easier than getting those snowsuits on. I was bursting to go to work every morning. The boys mimicked my work ethic like fledging Puritans: Teddy at two dashing joyfully up the stairs to "go work now." Hunter back from preschool announcing, "I'm going to write a book. It's going to be about cars and trucks.

I'm going to write it with a pencil. And I'm going to call it *Mrs. Fox.*"

No one was more pleased with herself than I as a new mother. Recently a friend from those days said: "I like you much more now." It is wonderful to be thirty. (Whenever I see the bright young kids in their twenties—those terrible years when you've left your family and have yet to form another—I remember not to be jealous.) But it is not always so wonderful to *know* people who are thirty. At thirty-two, I brimmed with the marvel of myself: for though a mother, I was not *my* mother. I had managed to be home with my children and still have what surely was a promising career. In the video of Teddy's christening party, I deign to be interviewed, feeling as glamorous as Princess Diana, in an enormous black straw hat and a copious, shoulder-padded red-and-white polka-dot dress that did not quite obscure my extra pounds as clearly as I thought it did. In another video, two of the cutest little boys in the world play with their blocks, probably saying the cutest things ever said— except nothing can be heard over the steady voice of their mother bragging about the movie that was going to be made (but never was) of her first novel.

Life was great. And so, in the bafflingly, deeply neurotic way that would become my signature—I decided to move.

CHAPTER SIX

I RETURN

"... AND THE BOYS CAN BIKE to Alcott House to see Amy's golden curl!" I proclaimed to Charlie one morning while still living in New York, as yet another irrefutable reason to move to Concord. It was an alluring vision, though wrong on at least three counts. The golden curl resided in England; the Alcott house was actually called Orchard House; and the boys, soon to decapitate their My Buddy dolls, would never know of Amy, let alone her golden curl.

Our first house in Concord—if we hadn't pulled out of the deal.

I'd been longing to move to Concord since visiting my parents a few Christmases before, when I'd bought Hunter and Teddy stocking presents from Woolworth's Five and Ten—the stimulant of my grasping childhood. Almost every day after school, I had roamed along the glittering aisles of fake diamond rings and dolls who could go to the bathroom and real birds in cages—craving. I had been taught as a child not to want *things*—as my mother and the Concord matriarchs would call anything new and unnecessary—with the predictable, adverse result. That afternoon I bought every toy truck in sight. As I left the store and stepped out on Walden Street, arms full of thin, breaking brown bags, a gentle snow was falling. The town had looked as beautiful and unreal as a town in a snow globe.

But it wasn't until the next year that my longing to return to my hometown became obsessive. Suddenly the Victorian house of my dreams, thirty minutes from Manhattan—where my sons had learned to walk, talk, and projectile vomit—meant nothing. Suddenly my best friends living nearby in the city, my fledgling career, and Charlie's rise at ABC News meant nothing. Suddenly being cool and wearing a leather jacket while nursing my baby in a Greenwich Village restaurant meant nothing—next to the thought of my children floating toy boats on the Concord River while my mother and I looked on. Not that ever, ever had I floated a toy boat, let alone with my mother, along the Concord River. I was conjuring an image of my childhood as sweet and erroneous as Louisa Alcott's in *Little Women*.

Charlie had yet to quit his job at ABC and the house in New York wasn't yet on the market, but nevertheless we had driven up to Concord "just to take a look around," my mother breathlessly joining us. "My friends are so jealous I have a daughter moving to Concord," my mother cried out, as we trooped in and out of houses we couldn't afford or couldn't fit into. The broker was a mother of my youth and she and my mother and I excitedly planned the monthly "at home" teas I was suddenly promising to hold (with an open invitation to all my mother's friends!), while Charlie smiled queasily. The next thing we knew, we'd put $25,000 down on a house in Concord we'd only seen once.

Then, just as Charlie and I were getting in the car to drive back to New York, my mother suddenly mentioned my novel, which she'd sanctioned by letter a month earlier, now saying worriedly, "It's awfully flip about Concord." My novel was not yet out. An hour later I had become so physically ill at the prospect of moving to Concord, Charlie had to pull over at a rest stop to call the realtor to see if we could get out of the deal. Soon my parents were paralyzed with fear at what their friends would think, the home owners being members of their country club, though my parents knew them only by sight. "Well, if they're members of the country club, they should be nice enough to give us back our money," Charlie said testily.

"I'm afraid you'll just have to buy the house and sell it again," advised the local lawyer, whose mother my parents knew. Furious with everyone, Charlie called the owners' lawyer directly and got us out of the contract, the country-club-member owners pocketing $5,000.

We not only bailed on the house, we bailed on the move to Concord, detouring to Cambridge, where my publication day—which I had been so migrainously awaiting, fearing exposure, world renown, and the burden of wealth—came and went in perfect stillness. The book sold a handful of copies, except in Concord, where it was a best seller. My parents were pleased. And so we sold our Cambridge house six months after we'd purchased it and bought the house on the river down the street from where I'd grown up.

Thus it was that—after a few glitches—I returned to my hometown, glowing with my third pregnancy and a fulsome, stupid happiness I have never known since.

TO THE SHOCK OF THE WORLD, if it had cared, I became a provisional member of my parents' country club. The Concord Country Club was the kind of inexpensive, keep-it-simple club that rich WASPs used to be so fond of; it had started as a golf course in the backyards of the Concord old guard in 1895, grudgingly added tennis courts to its new location many decades later, and was still, in the 1990s, without a bar or restaurant. Everything was labeled historic in Concord that possibly could be, and the Concord Country Club was, I was now (erroneously) informed, "the second country club in America."

My parents, who had always belonged to a country club as if it were a dire necessity, had joined in 1957 as a matter of course. There my family had played quarrelsome tennis with little skill and much male racket-throwing on hot August weekends, the club ghostlike, most of its members at summer houses. There, as the only girl from public school, I had stood awkwardly at the country club eighth-grade dinner dance, silenced by the celery string stuck between my front teeth. There, as a teenager, with the righteous bitterness of the age, I had taken my grungy brothers and friends onto the tennis courts—looking like mass murderers with Charlie Manson hair and dirty, cut-off corduroys— as yet another sure-fire protest against the war in Vietnam.

Nothing much had changed at the Concord Country Club, where the young girls and old girls played golf and tennis in the weekday sun in jaunty skirted outfits; nothing had changed except for me. No longer large-kneed and gangly, I billowed with continuing motherhood, too happy and too pregnant even to pretend to have a career. I was a housewife with a babysitter to help her with the goody bags—for a brief moment one of the privileged unearning suburban mothers I had once avoided—watching my little boys learn tennis and swimming and golf, a small chunk of fast-dwindling house-loan credit in my theoretical pocket. As I sat in the pool dressing room helping Hunter and Teddy get into their neon bathing suits, I inhaled the chlorine and the swimming pool din that brought me back to my own wading pool days, after my mother had come home from the hospital and I had been so happy. And now, my children could be happy too.

With another wrench of nostalgia, I joined, for an annual $150, White Pond, where I had swum as a child before the Concord Country Club built its pool sixty stingy years after its establishment, just as I turned thirteen and was too self-conscious to be seen in a bathing suit. White Pond, where Goldie Hawn and Kurt Russell, here to film a movie one humid summer, were turned away with their kids because they didn't have a sticker on their rented car. The first time I brought my boys to White's, at the end of a hot day in July, I spotted a high school classmate, Candy Santino, whom I hadn't really known then. But now, I was ecstatic, calling out, "Candy!!!" And there were Candy Santino's two boys, the same age as mine, what a coincidence!—though certainly they were a full twenty pounds larger in size, dwarfing my boys, who suddenly looked anemic. I walked my boys up to Candy's scions and beamed at them as they played on the shore. I remembered, with yet another swell of the heart, that the reason I had come back to this town was to send the kids to a good public school with a wonderful mix of backgrounds—to a place where, for a time at least, the social classes would not seem to exist. It would be a few years before I realized the class system in Concord had reversed, the farmers' families, having sold their land to developers for millions, now wintering in Arizona.

And Candy Santino's boys—could they really be only four and five, surely they were seven and eight, those big, tan, beefy, strong boys with buzzed hair? (Mine, slathered with sunblock, were English-white and Beatle-mopped.) "Hi," I said brightly, introducing Hunter and Teddy. The Santino boys ignored us, intent upon their game. The game was cutting worms in half and watching them squirm tortuously to death. My darling pale boys watched with open mouths of horror—or was it deep admiration? I thought of Hunter in preschool ("The politest boy in school," said Mrs. Fox, because his whole first year, Hunter only said three words, "please" and "thank you") and how terrified he'd been of Jake the bully, and then one day he'd asked if he could have Jake over. "The *bully*?" I'd asked. "Yes," Hunter had whispered, "I like the bully."

"Well," I said cheerily now to those mammoth youngsters who had not acknowledged our presence, "the boys and I agree, it's one thing to kill animals that invade our houses, but we think it's unfair to kill them outside in nature, their home!" The Santino boys looked up at me briefly and blankly, then chopped another worm.

And then it was September, and my heart sang with the remembered joy of new beginnings. For just as the excitement of Christmas is reborn with the advent of one's own children, so the optimism of September is reborn. Especially on this September day when Hunter was to begin kindergarten, clutching his Ninja Turtle and dressed in green incandescent pants ending in elastic at Velcro sneakers with blinking soles, the uniform of the day. Hand in hand, we crossed our pretty, quiet street to the bus stop directly opposite our house. The children stood mirthlessly, concentrating on their places in line, as the parents chattered easily among themselves, laughing at apparent jokes. For we were proud to be hovering, proud to be unlike our own less anxious parents—who had shooed us out the door to bus stops with 25¢ for lunch, instead of themed fanny packs filled with healthy treats.

I accompanied the rest of my morning with complacent humming until the stroke of noon. Then, with a spirited step, I recrossed the street to await the triumphant return of my eldest son, gone forth those three hours into a mysterious world beyond my protection. I settled my bulk comfortably on an old stone wall under a perfect blue sky. Pregnant in Concord, I felt absolved of all my sins. The warm sun and my seventh month of gestation filled me with a storybook peace. I was as thrilled with myself (and just as fat) as the always-right, always-in-the-same-polka-dot-dress Mama in the Berenstain Bears. "Mama! Mama!" Teddy and Hunter invariably called out to me in the hardware store, to my great embarrassment. But this day I did not care. I *was* Mama, waiting for the yellow school bus to lumber toward me down Bear Country Lane.

The school bus lumbered toward me, hissing with an evocative sigh to its stop. I rose with an expectant, effervescent smile. And then Hunter got off, and said to me, his terror making it his longest sentence ever, "Mommy the bus driver yelled at me for not sitting down soon enough but I couldn't help it because the other kids were standing in front of me." I promised him with the indulgent smile of one who still believed in justice that the bus driver would not yell at him again. Who would ever yell at Hunter, who was so intent on doing the right thing it would take him four weeks to summon the courage to buy milk at school, because he wanted to have the exact change and had not yet ascertained its cost? ("Hunter, did you happen to find out how much the milk is?" I asked casually day after day, until finally he answered solemnly, "It's either forty *bucks* or forty *cents*." "What do *you* think?" I asked gently. Hunter pondered. "Forty bucks?") The next morning I watched him climb onto the bus, only to be trapped in the middle of a group of kids clogging the aisle. I watched the bus driver snap the doors shut like the matron of a correctional facility, then Thurberesquely turn her bulk around, opening her mouth to yell. Suddenly my body was flooded with the fear I felt for my child, rushing through my veins, draining them of their last euphoric molecule, obliterating all the deep and shallow joys of my life—the wallpaper that just arrived for the new powder room, the view of the river out my window, my perfect marriage—nothing existed next to this fear that my son would be yelled at. Through the closed glass door of the bus I saw the noiseless scream emanating from the driver's open mouth and shooting down the aisle at him. Helpless, I turned away. Burning through the haze of delusion was the first glimmer of truth: that no matter where I lived, my children would feel the same pain I did; that no matter what I told them, it would probably be a lie.

CHAPTER SEVEN

MARMEE AND UTOPIA

I HAD ENVISIONED CONCORD, I realize now, as a kind of utopia, where I would give my children the perfect childhood. Even a trip to the dentist on a brilliant October afternoon was to be a glorious adventure—with balloons and stickers and bubble-gum flavored toothpaste! "I don't know," said a baffled Teddy as we'd left, "going to the dentist wasn't *that* great." But to me, it had been great.

The drafty pre-Revolutionary farmhouse in whose cramped quarters Bronson Alcott's "consociate family" froze, starved, and nearly died—in order to perfect mankind.

Concord has been inspiring utopias with mixed results ever since the first Puritans came to convert the Indians in the name of Christ, only to kill them later, also in the name of Christ. Thoreau built utopia in the Walden woods— near to his parents' house but not too near—where for the only two years of his tubercular life he was never sick. Emerson hoped to create an intellectual utopia, inviting shiftless friends to move into his house. Hawthorne found a brief paradise during his honeymoon at Concord's Old Manse. And then—there was Bronson Alcott.

One Sunday, on one of those piercingly beautiful fall afternoons that make you despair of ever having the courage to leave New England, Charlie and I drove ten minutes west to visit the site of Bronson's failed utopian community. At Fruitlands, the utopians vowed to wear no cotton (because of slavery), drink no milk (because the milk belonged to the calf), eat no meat and wear no leather (because animals had "a right to the pursuit of happiness"). Even the worms possessed equal rights, Bronson decided, ceding to them his scant apple crop. "Poor Fruitlands!" Louisa wrote thirty years later. "The name was as great a failure as all the rest."

Still, it was hard to blame Bronson for his optimism as we turned onto a spectacular rise of land overlooking the brilliant Nashoba Valley—where, centuries ago, Concord's "praying Indians" had been transplanted so hopefully by their Puritan converters, only to perish; and where today Concord's more privileged youth learn to ski almost as soon as they learn to walk. At Nashoba Valley, at the too-old age of ten, I had been ignominiously dragged by sodden rope tow up the kiddie slope on my tummy—only to return thirty years later with equal ignominy to chat nervously inside the lodge, trying so hard to get another mother to like me I did not hear the loudspeaker outside bellowing for one straight hour, "Would Teddy Stuart's mom please come to the information booth!!"

But that day, the scene was as serene as Bronson fancied himself, and gazing before me, I found it impossible to imagine the Christian Indians suffering there more than three hundred years ago, or the Alcotts some two hundred years later. We were directed down the steep path of the postcard-perfect green hill, past transplanted historic buildings and a fairy-tale well, to the drafty, pre-Revolutionary farmhouse in whose cramped quarters Bronson Alcott's "consociate family" had frozen and starved and nearly died—in order to perfect mankind.

The theory at Fruitlands was that its (male) inmates would themselves determine where duty lay: in the fields, inside philosophizing, or out in the world recruiting. One can guess where that led. When it came time to harvest the barley, there was not a man on the place. The women—that is, Marmee and the girls—had to rush out in a storm to salvage what they could. As the first winter approached, with debts mounting and food running out, Bronson began spouting "madman" schemes of joining a commune that believed in free love, asking his crying girls what they thought of family separation, as Louisa "prayed God to keep us all together." Finally, Marmee had her brother pull his financing and took her sad, sick, starving, freezing children away to nearby friends. Bronson tagged along, announcing his plan to starve himself to death. But even at this he would fail.

When I'd looked up the hill that Sunday from the farmhouse to the panorama that will in perpetuity remain Fruitlands—endowed by a wealthy spinster, Clara Endicott Sears—I felt the semi-euphoric life-weariness that is the gift and the curse of middle age. I thought of Marmee, who had dreamt her husband would save the world, and then had had to save her children from her husband; of my mother, vowing she would never abandon her children as her own mother had; of my own hopes that my children would feel they belonged in a town where I had never fit in. Memories of life already lived filled me with such weight, that I, the daily jogger, could not make it up the unrelenting hill. Suddenly the story of the Alcotts was all too much.

For by then I had been inside the house. Miss Sears wrote that it was easy to mock the Fruitlands experiment, but that something should be said for having ideals in any time. It sounded like something a rich Unitarian might say. It was all very well for Bronson, farm bred and a healthy forty-three, to subsist on apples and water, but what of his four girls, ages two to twelve, denied milk and protein? Fruitlands had been a laughingstock from the beginning, but when I left the farmhouse, the last thing I wanted to do was laugh.

By then I had seen "the old-fashioned bonnet" that was Marmee's signature, striped, grimy, and lovingly preserved; I had read the note that Louisa left inside her mother's worn change purse, saying *This is the purse Marmee always used.* I had read the letters written by Marmee to Louisa after Marmee had instituted a family post office so the girls would have a private outlet to express their unhappiness. I had seen the narrow bed where Marmee and Bronson had contemplated celibacy, separation, and free love. I had climbed to the spooky attic room where the girls had cried themselves to sleep.

But mostly I had seen Marmee's striped bonnet behind glass. Though it was a clinging neurotic love, though Marmee had once given a picture to ten-year-old Louisa of a little "industrious" girl taking care of an ailing mother, saying that it was her dream for Louisa—still Marmee's love moves me more than any other fact of the Alcotts' life. Despite her idolizing of her husband, Marmee put her children first. And suddenly I realized that what had drawn me to *Little Women* as a child, and still drew me, was the desperate but noble attachment between a mother and her daughters.

When I could not make it up the hill, I stopped at the art museum that contained Miss Sears's collection of primitive portraits. But the first portrait displayed was not primitive; it was a portrait of Miss Sears's mother as a young woman. And I knew that Miss Sears had preserved Fruitlands not for Bronson, but for his wife.

CHAPTER EIGHT

THE MOTHERS WHO WERE TOO GOOD

THE SAME STRIVING FOR PERFECTION that built the Puritans' utopias in New England long ago is still here, driving its town mothers to fight off the garish hordes. Whenever you pass through a beautifully quaint New England town crying out, "Oh, how unspoiled," never forget that bloodbaths have been waged to keep it so.

Our third year in Concord, Charlie and I decided to

Our first house in Concord, which I would soon ditch like an insensitive lover beating a fast retreat.

enlarge the porch and paint the house. This might have been a simple enough proposition in most parts of the world, but nothing was simple in our perfect New England town. It turned out that our house, though relatively young and a mile from the town center, was in a designated historic district because it was across the street from a house built in 1763. Therefore, we soon learned with trepidation, we could not paint the outside of our house or plant a bush or put up a picket fence or do anything visible from the street without the town's written permission.

And so one frosty morning, a brigade of ferociously frill-less women in L.L.Bean coats descended upon us. These were the women of the Concord Historic Districts Commission and just about every other commission in town (on the census they list their occupation, terrifyingly, as: *volunteer*). Charlie and I stood on the second-floor landing, trembling at the sound of their old car doors slamming, shuddering as they marched toward our door. Charlie had trouble breathing; a vein throbbed above my left ear. Suddenly we doubted ourselves: why *were* we spending money on our house instead of saving it? Why, for that matter, had we never saved anything? These women had saved throughout their entire lives—they were saving now. They carpooled to get here; they don't touch the guest towels in my powder room, but emerge shaking their hands dry. They've saved on clothes, on face creams, on Scotch tape, on Christmas presents, on wrapping paper, on demonstrations of affection. I dash down the stairs and fling the door open, leaning toward them with feigned enthusiasm, almost kissing them, as if they were aunts at Thanksgiving. I give them home-ground coffee (having ground the beans at six-thirty a.m.) and homemade coffee cake on my wedding china (Lenox Morning Blossom, but nobody cares). "Decaf?" they ask sharply (they even save on the air they breathe). "But certainly," I lie fulsomely. The cake is scarfed down with a second glass of juice ("Won't need lunch," the ladies mutter); the plates are brought to the sink, the napkins returned, smoothed and unsoiled. I trail behind them as they march out the door and stand before our shabby-gray house, two halves of a sloping roof framing the front door like the ears of a forlorn puppy. "I just don't see why you have to change *anything*," grumbles one woman. "I don't either," says another. Inside my house I see a shadow slither furtively down the back stairs and out the back door. Charlie has escaped.

But not for long. For we live in a town held hostage by such women. In our neighborhood we watch them grow from fledgling into seasoned hawk. And when a storm takes down our arborvitae hedge, one passing by remarks to Charlie that our hedge wouldn't have fallen if he'd thought to trim it more often. "Merrie Knox said I should have known better!" Charlie says, roaring into the house, his Saturday ruined. But he doesn't roar to Merrie, O cruelly deceptive name. Bunny, Perky, Baby, Smudgie, Cricket, Teeny, Twinky, Jab (with mother Jib!). Tough old birds to the world, they cultivate girlishness with each other, exchanging $5 birthday presents ("You shouldn't have!") or Cheerios cooked in the oven as cocktail treats (for even their *Mayflower* ancestors knew how to drink). The thought that counts is the creed. But what is the thought but to save at anyone's expense, to show you are thrifty, to be deemed good rather than to do good? Who were your mothers that you can indulge no one except your dog? "Oh when, oh when will my mother die!" complains a seventy-year-old Bunny at a party. Her mother is ninety-three and lives on and on, still unfairly blaming her daughter for her baby cousin's accidental death sixty years before. For the truth is: these Bunnies and Crickets deserve commendation, even love, for they have survived their own disapproving mothers.

"I JUST THINK that Jiffy Montgomery is so attractive," my mother said one hot day as I stood in the country club parking lot, sweating through some kind of hopelessly jury-rigged outfit from my office days. The country club had a no-jeans dress code that threw me into a panic every day at eleven-thirty before I went to pick up the boys from golf-tennis-swim, praying I would not have to get out of the car. But that day my mother had been there.

Together we gazed at Jiffy, crisp and boxy in pimiento Bermuda shorts and Lanz flower-print blouse, hands on hips and deep in thought, eyeing the entrance of the country club swimming pool with consternation. Recently it had been announced that Jiffy had become an officer of the pool committee. Jiffy might have been a member of my mother's generation with her short set-to-withstand-the-elements hairdo, but in fact she was my age, or perhaps younger. Jiffy wore themed pictorial sweaters and was a member of the Seeds and Weeds, and outside her house I'd seen the long line of badly parked cars from which emerged Foggy Brice and Blinky Foster, cradling their creations. I wanted to cry out to my mother, "Why can't you wish I were Mother Teresa or Katie Couric or Maya Angelou?" Anyone but Jiffy. If Jiffy was the bar, I could not reach it.

I had come back to Concord to improve upon my parents' child rearing, at the same time wishing to gain my parents' approval for doing so. For just as Louisa May Alcott had chained herself to her parents' approval, just as Henry Thoreau had railed so self-righteously against the townspeople of Concord, all the while unable to leave them—so, apparently, correcting my parents' mistakes had no point unless I corrected them in front of my parents' eyes and won their praise for demonstrating to them what they'd done wrong.

Within a mile of my house, my parents lived, worrying that if we fixed up our house too much it would hurt the feelings of the former owners. My mother made flower arrangements with a Hollywood theme ("Steel Magnolias," she told me over the phone, "with tinfoil for leaves!"); my father, long retired, played paddle tennis on cold winter evenings and affably delivered meals to the (sometimes younger) elderly for the Council on Aging. My parents were active at town meetings and joined discussion groups at the Unitarian Church, where everyone agreed fiercely about everything, and they were a far more vibrant part of the town than I would ever be, or would wish to be.

Charlie and I had thought we could raise our kids without the time-proven tool of guilt that had been employed by New England Protestants ever since they had braved the Atlantic in a leaky boat so their children would stop enjoying themselves. Despite the initial appearance of Charlie's tacky 1970s apparel, I had not married a thug, or someone, as my parents would have put it, "from a different back-

ground." Though Charlie said "irregardless" and sometimes wore a Ban-Lon body shirt to work and a Roto-Rooter
baseball cap all weekend long to show he was a man of the
people, he was not a man of the people but a man of my
people. And he too had been weaned from milk bottle to
gin bottle on the icy Calvinistic belief that you were either
good or bad, with no recourse to the comfort of priest or
confessional.

Growing up, we'd been taught the responsibility of daily
duties and the shame of a job left undone. But for our kids
there was no long list of chores stuck on the refrigerator
door. No raking the lawn or cleaning the bathroom on Saturday mornings or taking turns doing the dishes after dinner. "What do you do to help around the house?" Hunter
was asked on a homework paper in the fourth grade, and
after much parental consultation, all we could come up
with was, "Carry my own skis."

Our mothers had worried that compliments would
swell our heads. When Janie McClintock and I ran for
Class Librarian in the fifth grade (librarian being so much
more feminine than president), we solemnly swore to vote
for each other, though it was a blind vote, because to
vote for oneself was conceited. After I had written "Janie
M." on my ballot, I'd looked up to see the dreamy look that

always came over Janie's sweet face when she peed, and wondered for one fleeting moment if Janie had complied.

But Charlie and I brought our kids up on "positive reinforcement," complimenting them from dawn to dusk, so that Teddy at four had flung the ancestral crystal to the floor because I said he looked "good" in his chicken-beaked rain coat, not "great." Week after week, I feigned excitement as I entered the boys' masterpieces in the drawing contests run by *Highlights* magazine for children, silently doubting that their renderings of daggers plunged into blood-dripping heads would win the prize. ("Home from the Front" I hopefully entitled one gory picture drawn after the Gulf War that happened to have an airplane, albeit with a bomb.) My parents had spanked their children for freshness and washed our mouths out with soap for cursing. We'd been fined half our allowance every week until (by some miracle of accounting) we'd paid for the cot we'd used as a trampoline. But for their infractions, my children were sat on a carpeted "time-out step" for five restful minutes with a fresh juice carton, so comfortably that a friend of Teddy's once begged to be punished that way.

Since I'd become a mother I'd found rules pouring out of me like lava. My mother's rules had governed chores and correctives. My rules were not to punish but to give my children the security that someone (their mother) knew what she was doing. "How could we ever have kids?" Charlie had asked a decade before, as he was leaving me after our first year of marriage. "You can't even drive to the store to get a gallon of milk without getting lost!" Now, defying even my own expectations, I dispensed wisdom all the day long, with the confidence of Solomon. "Only one soda a week unless substituted for dessert after fruit," would roll off my tongue effortlessly in response to a query. "My father's kind of silly," I heard seven-year-old Hunter tell a friend, "but my mom's *really* smart." Whereas Teddy, learning lawyering, had skimmed by me with a full plate of sweets, with the murmured explanation: "cookie of the day, legal snack, dessert cereal, brownie from yesterday, *Strawberry* Crunchies."

I wanted my parents to say, "Isn't it great that Sally spoils her children with stocking presents that fill the living room at Christmas! Isn't it marvelous that she can write a novel about Concord, embarrassing her parents, and still live here!" "How great that Sally dresses like a member of the homeless and refuses to meet our friends we know she would *love* because they are the same age!" As the decade progressed and I began the march toward the half-century mark, I still craved my parents' approval, yet found myself unable to do the requisite thing to gain it—to dress correctly (or even decently, without the big wet spot over my bosom where I have hurriedly swiped at a tomato sauce spot) and write books about history, or landscape gardening, or about *anything* but what I always ended up writing about: my parents.

But back when my mother was alive and my children were not yet teenagers, the struggle was worth it: though I trembled before each parent-teacher conference, dressed as if I had never had sex lest the teacher disapprove of me; though I added twice the canned pumpkin filling to the cookie batter as I "helped" at Halloween Fun Day, producing cookies that glowed in the dark; though I hid behind bushes whenever a book or article came out; though the slightest lift of my mother's brow could send me crawling to my room—still there was hope that one day, someday, the light of an approving smile would shine upon me.

HOW HAPPY I almost was at Teddy's first-grade back-to-school night, as I sat on that short, wobbly chair in an overwarm, overparented, fluorescent-lit classroom, identical to the one my first-grade teacher, Miss Flora, had ruled so benevolently thirty years before. Here were the same squat, mullionless windows that cranked open only a few inches and never quite closed, so that you fried on hot days and shivered on cold. Here was the same blackboard with the same soothing, confident *swish* and *dot* as Teddy's teacher chalked her name in perfect teacher-handwriting. Here were the same impossibly shiny linoleum hallways leading past clanging metal lockers to recess and the pulsating blacktop, the battlefield of childhood, a tiny pebble of which still resides in my knee today. First grade! Miss Flora, in her flowered, synthetic grandmother dress, one hundred years old but probably forty, stern at first, but later kind, the absolute center of our helpless, short lives with her gentle rules and just rewards. For Miss Flora, we would salute the flag and ask the Lord's forgiveness for our *tres-passes* (and wonder again why the Lord cared so much if we wandered into somebody's else's woods).

And now I sat at Teddy's tidied desk with his carefully printed invented-spelling message, below the crayoned rendition of the family, with the yellow-haired boy in its center (Teddy) mysteriously taller than the shrimpy brown-haired boy squashed to one side. "Hunna thinks I'm stupid!" Teddy had wailed at one and a half about his older brother, defining forever the psychological hurdle of his life. Teddy at four had broken away, announcing, "Mommy, I like the rough music better," rejecting Raffi's ruinously toneless "Let's Do the Numbers Rumba!" that I had so dutifully, on pediatrician's advice, subjected Hunter to from the cradle—so that his second-grade report read: "With a great deal of time and effort, Hunter's sense of rhythm *might* improve." Hunter's first weeks of first grade had been an unmitigated disaster; once so well adjusted in half-day kindergarten, he had been suddenly burdened, returning home with brow as black as Snoopy's flying baron, until we'd finally figured out that he'd been trying to be perfect for too many hours in a row ("But I don't *want* you to be perfect," I had lied). But Teddy had breezed into first grade already cool, looking like a rock star in a black T-shirt as he scowled pensively ahead at the bus stop—until he opened his mouth to say, "Purple is my *second* favorite Shark Bites color." Teddy was "the most social boy" his teacher had ever met, a bright light in the classroom, except, frowned Ms. Groe (pregnant with her first son of two), when he had led the laughter in the doll corner.

Enjoy it while it lasts, I should have been thinking at Teddy's back-to-school night. All around me glowed posters of six-year-old self-portraits, pushpinned to the bulletin board, each listing the child's many sterling attributes, glittering with potential. At six, every child in this pristine town is beautiful to look at and talented to boot, and every parent knows it. I certainly knew it, as I breathed in the heady atmosphere of first grade: minuscule plants in labeled egg cartons poking up hopeful green shoots; the class gerbil, guaranteed to die before Christmas vacation, quietly, fatalistically stuffing himself to the gills ("Emily has expressed interest in bringing home the class newt for summer," I would read in horror five years later); the book corner with Corduroy still waiting, buttonless in the shop window, and Mama Bear, preaching her lessons, arms akimbo or wagging a finger—yet somehow comforting with her simplistic justice, the modern Marmee. *This is it, this is why I came back,* I think as I look around me, *this is what I am thankful for, even exultant.*

Exultant, but also nauseous. Sick, since the moment I'd stepped through the classroom door and seen the other parents: the men in their business suits, all legs in their tiny seats, smiling blankly, blandly, needing a drink; their wives, fluttering, pleased to be seen in their element, dressed brightly in bulky knit sweaters and unflattering slacks, leaping to the fore to sign up for Pumpkin Festivals and Teacher Appreciation Breakfasts. As the long sign-up sheet of volunteer activities makes the rounds, a migraine hits me between the eyes like a bullet in Bambi's mother. I long for an ambulance to take me away, to be rolled through the crowd on a soft gurney with clean white sheets, the para-

medics with their firm "excuse me" shunting the other
mothers aside. But instead I watch the other mothers chatting away with one another, so much to say, bustling with
enthusiasm and signing up here and signing up there, these
college-trained women my age who have given up their careers for their children. This is the first town I have lived in
as an adult where most of the women, rich and otherwise,
don't work for a living. They are nicer, less pretentious than
at the tony private preschool of my friends in Cambridge,
where the mothers worked full time with long wine-filled
lunches, joyfully dropping their kids off for the day, dressed
to the nines with real jewelry, sorting out the other mothers
by the fashionableness of their address.

And yet I am far more frightened of the bustling, competent Concord mothers who have become the leaders of
the elementary school, rising like cream to the top of the
parent groups, as they had once risen in their professions.
I, on the other hand, had been too anxious for approval to
move up the ranks when I'd been an advertising copy-
writer. And, when I read the magazine article on what
makes girls grow up to be successful in corporate America,
I sighed to realize that Emily—so soft she feels a tear rising
on behalf of the sugar bowl when it chips—would probably not become CEO of a Fortune 500 company.

I know that the world needs these leaders among women

more than it needs me. But still I spot them with terror from my kitchen window as they come in for landings at my mailbox in their armored, weaponlike vehicles. Hurriedly, they push in the announcement "We need more cakes!!" for the cake raffle being organized for the school carnival, that arrives too soon every June, like a six-month dentist appointment. The school carnival, which I must attend in the white heat for each child and face the band of mothers who do not know me because in the whole year I have only volunteered for one measly activity. Perhaps that is why every single year I am asked, a message left on the phone machine for my children to hear, to be the carnival's "Jailor," to wear a policeman cap and arbitrarily "arrest" other parents, who then must be bailed out by carnival tickets. And every year I crawl to the phone, over the bodies of my disappointed children, to refuse.

Who are these women who computerize spreadsheets for play-group assignments and tennis-lesson carpools; who orchestrate mailings and refreshments and committees for the PTA; who never have a minute to spare because they are running off to help the teacher (who does not wish to be helped, surely! but left alone) in the classroom, in the library, in the learning resource center. Who are these mothers who cry with joy when the children return home with their assignment for the class Colonial village, making fabulous fir tree forests cut from green foam material they just happened to have stored in a closet—while I can't seem to cut out a paper crown for five-year-old Emily from a piece of computer paper. "Oh why oh why," Emily cries out, despite her never-complaining self, "couldn't I have a creative mother?"

And though I know I am far from alone, that many other mothers, kinder women than I and more fragile, cower too at the sight of these competent amazons, though I have one panicked friend who has checked herself several times into the ER on her days to parent-help—I cannot reach out to them or they to me, lest we brand ourselves by association. Instead of reaching out, I thrust a knife into the hearts of my fellow sufferers, one-upping even the competent mothers, as I march to the bus stop one December morning bearing a Christmas present for the bus driver.

For three bright and sunny days I lie in my bedroom with the soft blue floral wallpaper, the shades drawn against the sparkling river, my head pounding even as I sleep, because I am afraid the other mothers from Hunter's second-grade class will reject me on the field trip to Great Meadows. And when finally the big day arrives, I hobble, with eyes squinting against the blinding sun, down mossy, pine-needled paths, as Hunter, secretly proud that his mother is there, charges around me with the five other boys under my supervision. "Look," I croak out with a weak, fake smile to mask my horror, "a snake." And Hunter and his friends scramble excitedly as I sneak a look at my watch. Only eight minutes have elapsed. "Where does the time go?" says another mother, a hundred hours later, when it is time to reboard the yellow bus. But Hunter is ecstatic; breaking rank, he holds my hand, because for this one day, his mother was like the other mothers.

CHAPTER NINE

GOD AND MOTHERHOOD

"WHY DON'T WE GO TO CHURCH? Kevin O'Dell's family goes to church," Hunter queried his second-grade year. Already I had denied Hunter a second year in the Cub Scouts (and Teddy *any* year in the Cub Scouts) after it was announced that mothers and sons would be spending the night on a real battleship. But denying my kids church took a kind of courage I did not think I could sustain. It seemed that every child and every parent in Concord rolled from

---

Trinity Church, built in the 1960s with a strong resemblance to the Howard Johnson's down the street.

bed on a Sunday morning to wince down orange juice on top of just-brushed teeth and microwave yesterday's coffee to a ruined boil and scrounge for something decent to wear—from the Catholic boy, in suit and tie and his brother's leather shoes, to the Unitarian matron, attractively graying, in loden vest, peasant skirt, and long turquoise earrings. Each and every one—the angry-red one-month-old baby, the boy in a dirty walking cast, the somnolent teenager coatless in the snow, the weekend-dopey father, the ever-alert mother, sometimes even the grandparents—rushed off to join the swirl of their grateful, happy, presumably God-fearing townspeople, calling out greetings as they streamed in and out of their various picture-book churches.

God was dead for all the friends I had left in New York, but in Concord He wasn't just alive, He was overbooked. Cars jammed end-to-end Sunday mornings, parked halfway up the sidewalk half a mile down Main Street. Preteens were driven in at eight a.m. to sing in gospel choirs, picked up and driven back again for afternoon and evening youth groups; parents clattered off mid-service to teach Sunday school classes, bookmarked Bibles under their arms; the Sunday program (its shell to be returned for recycling) was no longer a pamphlet but a tome, containing page after page of activities—from Marvelous Mondays, to feminist knitting groups, potluck suppers, and Make a Difference Sundays. Daily e-mails were shot off to parents from church headquarters, asking for volunteers. In Concord, there was no day of rest for anyone, even the Lord.

Except, apparently, for me. On Sunday mornings, I hide upstairs while my boys in their truck pajamas watch their friends being dashed off to Sunday school by sprightly dressed mothers in low heels. Danny McGuire will trot out once again the tried (and not-so-true) sin of stealing his brother's Legos to appease his Catholic confessor, and Danny McGuire will emerge, despite the lie, guiltless, free as a bird to cheat and kick and hit and commit all the small sins of boyhood the rest of the week. But the childish sins of my boys accumulate week after week, one tiny transgression on top of the other, shading their every joy. I have told them they are good, even when they do "a hurtful thing," but who's going to listen to me? Why put a quarter in the swear box I instituted, after Teddy overhears me talking on the phone: "Mommy, you swear with your friends just for fun!" Yes, I miraculously know (because I have instituted them myself) the myriad rules that constitute our domestic moral code—a decreed amount of fruit to be consumed before dessert, sugary cereal permitted on Saturdays only, and so forth—but where am I on Sunday morning, when all Concord motherhood arises? Cowering under my comforter, in scanty nightie and unwashed face, dripping drops of instant coffee on "In Step With," the gossip column by James Brady in *Parade* magazine. ("It's amazing how well he's done for himself, considering. . . ." my mother had remarked once, getting him mixed up with the guy who got shot during the assassination attempt on Ronald Reagan.) What was wrong with me, anyway? Why couldn't I give my kids the comfort of a communal God?

AND YET—who had ever liked (let alone, loved) going to church? Certainly not I or my parents and siblings in the 1960s, when my family had mechanically gone to Trinity Church for the interminable hour before the inevitable roast beef midday dinner. We had plowed through the same old hymns—my brothers and fathers harmonizing competitively, I counting how many more verses to go— and prayed to God, on the hard kneeling benches, that the sermon to come—polite, droning, and irrelevant—would, like all earthly afflictions, soon pass. Just as its "relevance" was being questioned, Trinity had, at great expense, built a cavernous edifice (which, with its massive Swiss chalet-style roof, strongly resembled the Howard Johnson's restaurant a half mile down the street), with the result that the church always looked three-quarters empty, and, despite a brief foray into guitar-playing in the aisle, increasingly was.

But now the fervor filled even my parents, long since switched over from Trinity to Unitarian First Parish, where liberal politics had replaced God in the equation. Gone was communion and praying on your knees and the Nicene Creed and Jesus rising from the dead and even having actually to attend church. Except now the parents and their friends looked forward to going to church, where the minister—charismatic, funny, a *Democrat*—once allowed he wasn't sure if he believed in God. And so ironically, First Parish—though an advanced, liberal, Unitarian Universalist bastion, quoting Thoreau left and right, welcoming all denominations and sexual orientations, etc.—had reverted back to its Puritan beginning when each member was on his own, constantly having to prove he was Elect. Out for all to see were the First Parishioners walking against modern-day slavery on a Sunday afternoon or circling Monument Square on a winter night holding candles to protest the war in Iraq. "It's nice that they're out there," Charlie said one evening, as we passed, "but why walk in Concord where everyone agrees with them?"

Once I had been avowedly apolitical—a blasphemy in the Unitarian Church—but now I lied to my mother when asked if I had registered to vote, guiltily saying yes, the guilt intensifying when she did a little dance. And when the formidable Mrs. Darling—high on the food chain of the parents' friends, with her attractive lawyer husband and four sailing-champ sons—had called one morning at eight to ask with confident superiority if I would hold a placard at the polls supporting Question 3, I trembled, not daring to ask what Question 3 was.

It was to First Parish I had obediently gone to christen my daughter, Emily, in a long Victorian gown from my mother's family. I prepared a large feast to serve on our beautiful deck, dressed the boys in the only sports coats I would ever buy them, and greeted godfathers and god-mothers flying in from out of town—only to learn, when we arrived en masse for the ceremony, that the Unitarian Church didn't have godfathers and godmothers, just "important people." After the fake christening, I avoided the church, only braving the disapproving eyes I imagined fall-ing upon me when I had to attend for the odd funeral. Even then, I ignominiously tried to slip out without shaking the hand of the extremely likeable minister, to whom I had once hastily garbled something about how going to church gave me migraines, with a forced chuckle, as if it were a joke we shared. My parents carefully refrained from commenting on my churchless-ness, except for the occasional, wonderful, transcribed sermon left hopefully on my front hall table.

I avoided phone calls from parishioners asking me to participate in the traveling potluck dinner parties or in the ceremonial signing of the membership book before the congregation. Our name was even bravely absent on the list of church contributors, until the boys hit middle school. Then a mild sum was sent in guiltily, as I signed each son up for the church's human sexuality class, notorious (once making national news) for its slide show featuring unattractive, unshaved men and women from the 1970s having sex in various adventurous and unflattering combinations (delaying the children's own experimentations, on the upside, for at least a year). "Back from sex class," Teddy and Hunter would say breezily when they returned. "It was pretty gross."

My retribution did not come until Emily joined the Unitarian youth group at age ten. "Wait till you have a daughter," my brothers had always said, "all the sins of your adolescence will be visited on you!" But so far my only punishment is Emily rising in the ranks of Liberal Religious Youth. Over I went dutifully, with snacks for forty-two, for a Sunday youth cabaret jam session, wondering why

a) the children even needed a snack during a mere hour and a half activity, and b) why the children couldn't just bring their own snack. As I waited nervously for the break before pouring out the forty-two Dixie cups of apple juice, a mother standing next to me, unable to contain herself any longer, had burst out in harsh whisper, "You only have five minutes. You have to start pouring *now*!" The man leading the rehearsal was no less disapproving of my anxious efforts to please. Running out of donut holes, I had dashed to buy more, only to be reprimanded when I returned that the children were now gathering in their improv groups and I was "interrupting the flow."

Fortunately, though a senior group leader, Emily never went to actual church. But then came the day when she approached me apologetically saying that the parents of the youth group were supposed to attend a certain Sunday service. Besides including a ceremony to commend the "youths" (as they were called), the service, as it turned out, featured a sort of grand finale to a "soil exchange" that had occurred, I learned, several months before. Apparently, parishioners—grown men and women—had brought in handfuls of dirt from their gardens and exchanged them (in buckets, one supposed) with one another. Now flowers resulting from the mingled soils were to be passed out to the congregation, *and,* we were assured, *even people who had not participated would be receiving flowers.* Down the nave came smiling parishioners bearing big baskets of glorious, stupendous blossoms. As the woman next to me and I were handed two scrawny little stems, she turned to me and whispered, "I guess they can tell who participated and who didn't."

CHAPTER TEN

THE BRAGGING YEARS

MY MOTHER WAS OFTEN ECSTATIC with a naïve optimism that took her far. "Life is all ahead of us!" she cried out excitedly one day at age seventy-four, as my father nodded, a cool eighty-one. Only my mother would have been optimistic about moving into an assisted-care facility. My parents had been happy as could be living on a small pension in a sunny apartment in Concord Center, having traded in their

---

The grand, if not very historic, assisted-living facility where, to the shock of all Christendom, my parents' decorator covered an entire living room wall with mirror.

ranch house in West Concord the year we'd moved to town. "We *much* prefer West Concord," my mother had declared often during the West Concord days but now it was, "I don't know how I *stood* that house for fifteen years!" against the little house to which she had once been so true. Back in the center of town, my mother had glowingly received the streams of friends passing through. My father had smiled his days down Main Street. "I saw your father downtown," everyone would say, and who could doubt them, for there he was: striding purposefully down the sidewalk, as handsome as a senior senator from Phoenix; standing at the crosswalk flirting sweetly with a spiffy, blond-gray divorcée in her sixties; gallantly holding open the large swinging doors of the Cambridge Trust Company for cranky Twinky Warren in her signature fur-balled sweater and canary-yellow rain hat bright against the blue sky.

But then, a few years after this happy move, my mother inherited a million dollars from her aunt Sarah. The next day she and my father appeared on my front porch trembling with excitement, announcing they had bought a "unit" in the fancy retirement complex under construction across from the country club, where the suites were named after the tony streets of Back Bay Boston. My mother was too young and my parents too healthy, they weren't ready, they loved where they were living, but now that they could afford it, they felt it was the right thing to do. Over they came day after day in the brown K-car with blueprints for the 600-square-foot apartment. Up we accompanied them in hard hats to see the view from the fourth floor still under construction, my parents finally screwing up the courage to switch from a unit with a parking lot view to another with a view of the woods. In a steely flash of independence, my mother blew $30,000 on a top-notch decorator, who to the shock of every WASP in Christendom, mirrored-over an entire living room wall.

Then they moved in. The problem began, as it always seemed to do, with the eating arrangements. My mother was resolved to eat dinner alone with my father every night, and so with head-splitting guilt she set about declining invitations to dine with the other residents. My parents would have given much to have been able to stay upstairs and eat Lean Cuisines in front of *The MacNeil/Lehrer NewsHour* instead of smiling through the drawn-out three-course dinner flourished before them each night, too buttery and too pureed—but their monthly fee included one meal a day. So my parents would dress for dinner and bravely go down to chat up the pretty waitress (with two baby girls living back in the Dominican Republic, weren't they cute?) and wave merrily—but not too merrily—at the rejected diners.

My parents' good friends were still too young to be at the retirement home and it was the more sickly of their acquaintances one would happen upon when my parents had chits to use up and invited us to dinner. We would be ushered in and there would be Mr. Cottingham—once so burly and outdoorsy in tall rubber boots and lumber jacket as he fished at his family's unelectrified camp in Maine—now with his arms stretched lifelessly across the table, facedown on the white linen table cloth, verging on death for all to view in the pale green dining room with the soft, expensive carpet and soundless gas fire and bowl of flowers for the latest departed inmates (who hadn't died, it turned out, but were celebrating birthdays).

It was a lovely, bright place, my parents' retirement home, but everyone knew it was the last stop before the Tunnicliffe Funeral Home. ("There's a turnover every five years," a staffer would say blithely to my parents after they'd lived there seven years.)

My mother feared the disapproval of just about everyone. Even Marcus, the maître d' of the retirement home restaurant, could vanquish my mother, or rather, *especially* Marcus. For some reason, this young, smiling, slightly aloof but hardly intimidating, perfectly mannered man of unknown ethnic origin (unknown, that is, to my parents, who dared not ask) held sway over many of the residents. "Where *are* you?!" my mother would gasp over the phone Easter Sunday. "It's ten-thirty and we're due in the dining room at eleven!"—though we were but five minutes away. Easter had become a big deal after we'd grown up. When we were children, the holiday had been dismissed as too commercial and we'd received no baskets or chocolate bunnies. Now in January it was, "*When* are you coming for Easter?" and bunnies at every place setting and jelly beans hidden about the apartment. "I suppose you'll have to bring Sam," my father sighed to my brother Johnny about his three-year-old grandson, who was worshipped by my parents and who perhaps of all of us might best have enjoyed the apartment's Easter egg hunt. But my parents had gotten the distinct impression that Marcus frowned upon small children in the dining room.

STILL, for a few precious years, before we began to disappoint one another, my parents had us, and we had them. For twenty years my parents had weathered the difficulties of their children—who were constantly dropping out, breaking down, or breaking up—and now suddenly down the street in the right house in the right part of town was a presentable daughter, with three presentable children young enough to pass for perfect, and a presentable husband from a similar background (meaning he drank).

I had my parents to approve of my glorious, if head-throbbing, life on a daily basis. For my happiness seemed to mean nothing unless it was constantly on view, as Protestant glory needs to be. In the afternoons I invited over other mothers, visiting aunts, the odd neighbor, whomever I could grab as witnesses to my good fortune, serving them tea on the second-floor deck, newly built, overlooking the yard and our playing children, an aerial view of my perfect motherhood. I bragged uncontrollably to the latest acquaintance, like the kid with the lowest self-esteem on the playground. To Kathy O'Dell, whose husband was already making so much money buildings couldn't be constructed fast enough to bear his name, I bragged, like the mouse to the lion, about how much the bushes cost in my front yard.

As if my bragging weren't enough, my parents pitched in—my parents, whose own parental brags had been thrown back so ignominiously in their faces with their own children, and who should have known better. My parents and their friends had once sniffed, "Concord is just not the same anymore with all these young people moving in and adding on to their houses." But we were those young people and no one was more pleased than my parents. Over to take a tour of the house came long-lost relatives and friends from the Marines, and New Haven, and New York, and Virginia, and New Hampshire.

My parents asked to bring people by so often that sometimes we had to deny them; and then I would catch sight of their brown K-car filled with the Hadleys from Chicago or Cousin Apples, related in some way past comprehension, my father driving slowly, hoping the earthy-toned car was camouflaged by the front hedge, then speeding up so they wouldn't be caught. The parents, as always, had been unable to resist buying the worst car on the market.

"The Greenes from New Haven are dying to come over, they haven't seen Sally since she was two years old!" my mother called one bright Saturday morning to announce. "She can't get out of bed, she's got a headache," Charlie had lied and I'd called out, "Tell them, no sneaking past the house!" An hour later I blithely opened the front door only to set eyes on the brown K-car lurking in front of the hedge. "Get back in the house, get back in the house!" Charlie had shrieked, pushing me through the door as if the Indians were attacking.

I MIGHT HAVE WELCOMED the Indians attacking, so guilty was I about my bragging. "Materialistic," "mercenary," "house-proud"—the damning adjectives of my parents' generation ran accusingly through my brain. And yet I queasily plowed on, too busy applying bank-borrowed money to our house to ponder the ever-fascinating question of when it would run out. But where had I learned this? Certainly not from her mother, who, though she'd grown up in glorious houses, had never expected or even wanted to live in one herself.

Marmee too, though she'd come from a family that had lived in mansions, wished only for a home where she didn't have to take in boarders. But even this was denied her.

Poor Marmee would always brim with anger against the people of Concord. She hated those who disparaged her husband for not working, on the one hand, but wouldn't give him a job in the town school, on the other; she derided as hypocrites the Concordians who neglected to feed the poor in town, as Marmee did out of her scant larder, and then looked down on the Alcotts for not attending church. What she really couldn't stand, of course, was that the Alcotts couldn't pay their bills, and everyone in town knew it.

After Marmee pulled the family out of Fruitlands, she never let go of the reins again. She rose above Bronson's ungrateful whines that he should have been single, that his family was to blame for Fruitlands' demise. She let him dither around, visiting other utopian communities. Finally, she acted. She took what Bronson's creditors hadn't claimed of her father's inheritance and bought her family their first house, Hillside. Unfortunately, the house was in the heart of what Marmee called "cold, heartless, brainless, soulless Concord," her "purgatory."

Martha Saxton, whose powerfully bleak biography of Louisa Alcott is nowhere to be found at the Orchard House bookshop, maintains that Marmee was basically in a full-scale depression the five years after Fruitlands. It would be hard for any of the Alcotts' more sprightly biographers to disagree, unless they were to argue that a clinical depression renders its victim unable to function. Because as God (and anyone in earshot) knew, Marmee was always functioning full-tilt—she didn't have much choice if she wanted her children to survive. Perhaps if she hadn't functioned quite so well, if she'd been able to indulge in a good solid self-pitying day in bed as her husband sometimes did, she might have been able to rest her overworked mother's mind.

And yet, while there are few historical figures I have more sympathy for than Mrs. Alcott, it must be said that feeling put upon seemed to have provided a kind of tortuous comfort zone for her. As Bronson so unsympathetically noted: she should have known what she was getting into when she married him. And while no one could have exactly foreseen the tumultuous life Bronson would lead his wife into—though perhaps a brief chat with his shell-shocked mother might have been instructive—still, surely deep down, Marmee must have gleaned that she would be sacrificed to this self-styled messiah. The sacrifice she could handle; what she couldn't handle was Bronson's not noticing.

But perhaps it was this complaining spirit that saved her. Marmee may have been depressed, but she was never quite in such despair that she couldn't shout it out. As opposed to my mother who turned her anger inward, Marmee had vented. She had waged a battle with her low self-esteem and emerged bloodied but victorious. Her disapproving father may not have believed in her—"He never loved me!" she claimed (a bit unfairly) when he hadn't left her more money than her siblings in his will—but her mother had. And so Marmee could believe herself worthy and her daughters worthy as well. This was the defining difference between my mother and Marmee. My mother's mother had told her she was bad, and Marmee's mother had to her that she was good. And so my mother was afraid of the world while Marmee was angry at it.

My mother's fear of what her Concord friends thought of her extended to what they thought of her daughter, as her representative. "We got on so well when you were in

New York!" she burst out once, for safely in New York, I had not been paraded before my mother's friends on a daily basis to be judged. Whereas in Concord, I could see my besieged mother trying to hide the thought processes in her mind when I arrived at some function with my brightly dyed red hair and ragged jeans. I should have known my mother was only mixing up her low sense of worth with her love for me. I should have noticed that I too worried about how it reflected on me as a mother when my own children appeared in public with lollipop bits stuck to their cheeks; or when Hunter, after all my glorious no-TV rules to promote reading, had answered the question on an elementary school worksheet—What do you do in your spare time?— "Watch TV."

When my mother huffed after Charlie and I had declined a dinner party invitation from a couple we didn't know who'd found out Charlie made documentary films— "Well, her husband is a selectman, so let's hope you don't need to get anything done in town!"—I should have laughed it off, instead of, so ridiculously, taking it to heart. But I too lived in a small town and cared too much about what other people thought.

CHAPTER ELEVEN

GOD AND REAL ESTATE

FOUR YEARS AFTER WE MOVED TO TOWN, Charlie and I were invited to the Concord Museum for a big gala and lecture about the history of Nashawtuc Hill. Nashawtuc means "between two rivers," and it was along the beautiful meadowland above the conjoining of the Assabet and Sudbury rivers that the Indians had fished and farmed with a great deal more success than their English usurpers would.

With sinking heart every morning, I would watch Charlie climb a ladder to paint the trim or wash the windows.

As a child, I had blithely ridden my bike down Squaw Sachem Trail, with no idea it honored a widowed queen of the Massachusetts tribe, a mother of five who became so powerful that other tribes sometimes sided with the English for protection from her. Nobody would have dreamed of purchasing Concord's six square miles from this formidable sachem until smallpox struck in 1633—a sign, the Puritan settlers had decided, that God was on their side in the real estate market.

But this was information I learned much later. At the time of the museum gala, despite the town's recent road signs translating the Indian names, the single thing I knew about the Concord Indians was Concord's cheery catechism that its name derived from the Puritan founders' serene transaction with them. And while my children had suffered through various units on town history, the only information I had ever gleaned from them was the surprise, announced at nine p.m., that I was supposed to bring in two dozen corn muffins for Colonial Town Meeting the next morning at eight-thirty.

For many years, Nashawtuc Hill has been one of the most expensive places to live in Concord, and the museum was thronged with a lot of very nice rich people eating hungrily from a hearty spread and drinking from a full bar. I was quite excited (and a bit drunk) when we all sat down to learn about the history of Nashawtuc Hill. How interesting it would be to finally learn about the Indians who had lived for so many thousands of years in the woods where my children and I rode our bikes. Instead, the grandmotherly, white-haired museum lady, whose salary, I suppose, was paid by those donations constantly and enthusiastically solicited in the mail, treated us to slides of various houses which had been built on the hill when its farmland had first been developed a hundred years ago, followed by slides of some very attractive new structures recently built by Elsie Range, one of the nicest people you'd ever want to meet and everyone's favorite architect. "A triumph!" I gushed to a friend who had organized the event, half meaning it. Because we had just bought a house on Nashawtuc Hill.

THE THOUGHT of moving always has and always will fill me with a piercing joy. My heart soars at the sight of a moving van down a street. When I am ninety-five, a wreath of shingles sluicing one eye, I will be tottering across a nursing home hallway to claim the still-warm dead man's room with the better view. For to not-move is to invite despair. To move is a new beginning, the surprise of hope, the sudden remembrance of anticipation, the race of sluggish blood—one is eleven again and out past bedtime on a summer night.

And so it was not the most surprising thing in the world that the minute I opened *The Concord Journal* one afternoon and saw that the price on a house on Nashawtuc Hill had dropped to the top of our credit limit, I called the realtor. Nashawtuc Hill has always been one of the prettiest, most convenient places to live in Concord, near the center, with turn-of-the-century houses overlooking long stretches of open land nobody seemed to own. The house on the hill had been on the market for two years. And yet until that moment, it had never occurred to me I could live there.

Usually, old houses abut busy roads, but the houses on the hill were insulated from the bustle of Main Street by a quarter mile of upward-winding road and stone bridges and wild meadows. The long-grassed lawns bordered not only the rivers but the woods around Egg Rock—the promontory from which the Indians had fished—where canoe paddlers can read the legend commemorating the native people of Concord. The six square miles that the Indians called Musketaquid had been purchased by the Puritans in a business-like manner for shell wampum, "hatchets, hoes, knives, cotton cloth, and shirts." Peaceful, the transaction may have been; legal, I'm sure the Puritan settlers assured themselves it was; but fair, even the self-appointed Chosen could not have believed.

In the woods hidden behind the rock, Thoreau had

scooped up arrowheads and nine-year-old Louisa May had played in the tiny time allotted her for childish pursuits. Stretched in front of the rock lie the "bogs," acres of purple-flowered wetland and river dividing the stately houses on the riverside of Main Street from their richer, less formal cousins on Nashawtuc Hill. During cold snow-less winters, the river overflow turns the meadows into a Currier and Ives scene of after-school skating, with the sky streaked orange above. Surely no child who has grown up here can ignore the evidence of God's benevolence. It was here Thoreau, Emerson, and Hawthorne skated together when the Hawthornes were honeymooning at The Old Manse, Sophia Hawthorne describing the scene. Thoreau executed "dithyrambic dances and Bacchic leaps on the ice," while Hawthorne "moved like a self-impelled Greek statue, stately and grave" and Emerson "closed the line, evidently too weary to hold himself erect, pitching head-foremost, half lying on the air."

But although I had biked and slid and skated and walked the environs of Nashawtuc Hill for over thirty years, I had never been inside any of its houses. Even my parents, who knew everyone, had no friends there: this was the neighborhood of Concord's oldest old guard, the self-effacing Elect, who appeared in bank lines in old clothes with the dirt of Concord's oldest gardens under their nails.

On Nashawtuc Hill, the money was so established and well-bred you never heard its rustle. Trucks had yet to screech and hiss up and down the patched macadam road to build on additions or install central air systems or roll down ready-made lawns and wood-chipped gardens. Giant lawn mowers and gaggles of foreign-born leaf blowers had yet to leap off flatbed trucks to disrupt the perfection of a fall day. The gangly gardens were still gangly, begun with 35¢ seed packets and a pound of sweat by owners who had had all the time in the world (and then some) and who had lavished on their plants the gentle care they would have considered indulgent to lavish on their young. Residents on the hill headed up land-trust walks and appeared at town meetings, but seldom at the country club, though most were members, and it was in their backyards the club had been founded. Living on Nashawtuc Hill was like getting your kid into a top college: the best thing to do was to keep your mouth shut about it. The first time Charlie would give Nashawtuc Road as his address, his local doctor would tear up, sniffing, "I always wanted to live on Nashawtuc Hill, but it just never worked out."

Even before I saw the Nashawtuc Hill house in the flesh, I knew, if ever I had known anything, that I would buy it—though I knew I shouldn't, though I knew it might all end in tears. I had known that I was too weak to resist the cozy beauty of the hill and the terrible lure of its desirability. Nashawtuc Hill meant success; after all my bridling as a teen against my parents as status seekers, apparently it was I who was the worst offender. And so I had known I would buy the house, with a sigh, just as Charlie had known it, with a sigh, just as even my hierarchical herding-dog Sheltie, Emma, had known it—Emma, as workaholic and conscious of status as the best Puritan. Emma had been a Puritan by the time she was four months old, shepherding my children hither and thither, lecturing me with disapproving barks followed by splashing retrieval when I wantonly allowed them to jump into a lake. Now it was as if she'd recognized the woodland smells and cool waters of Nashawtuc Hill as an Elect life. Earlier I had happened to take Emma on a walk up Nashawtuc Hill instead of her usual walk down the sidewalks of Main Street, and that had been the end of her usual walk, though Emma was a creature who craved routine even more than I. The next day, she had balked as we started down Main Street. I had pulled and pulled on her leash, while she, like a cartoon dog, had dug in her heels, standing stock-still, refusing to budge until, at last, I took the left, up the wildish delights of Nashawtuc Road.

I sighed as I drove the car up the hill to look at the house because I knew in my heart that moving here would be an act of hubris, that I was the fake thing and the people here were the real; that I would be forever waving my arm into the air, while the people here had long ago been called upon. I sighed because I knew that if I were a good person at all, if I cared for my husband or the peace of family, I would resist.

But then I reached the house, there on the top of the hill where I had sledded as a girl, and Henry and John Thoreau, and Louisa and Anna and probably even poor little agoraphobic Beth Alcott had sledded too. Here, surely the last sachem of this heaven-on-earth had stood with her new husband in his new cotton suit and watched the sun set on her old kingdom. I looked at the dilapidated house leaning out over the hill as if it were about to fall flat on its face. I walked inside, where each room was a tired tribute to the 1970s, with recessed lighting, and a pebble-filled planter running along the long wall of the Victorian dining room, and a stuffed parrot swinging on a string in the jungle-wallpapered powder room, and floors covered in wall-to-wall crew-cut shag, and toilets with rusted bowls. But the staircase swept up gracefully past leaded-glass windows, and almost every room faced the sweep toward the river below. And the midday sunlight shimmered, hovering in the air, as if through a prism.

Thus it was that, after four storybook years in our first

Concord house, we needlessly left it and moved a quarter mile up to the house on Nashawtuc Hill. We left the house where the sun streamed in from four exposures, where Emily had been beamed down from heaven, where Hunter and Teddy had flown so adventurously with their friends on a cable over a wading pool that, I learned later, had been laboriously filled with pee. We left the house where my mother and I had drunk afternoon tea before the fire, high on our briefly coinciding dreams, before the short sad years of mutual misunderstanding would begin.

"Change houses, not spouses," Charlie and I weakly joked. (And it was hard *not* to change houses when the banks had become so nice suddenly about not requiring that old stickler of income verification.) Oh, I had loved my refurbished farmhouse, but now the glow was gone, the honeymoon over, the bloom was off the rose and the petals off too, and as I hastened to ditch the house, I was like the least sensitive lover beating a fast retreat, unable to conceal my joy and relief at the release.

In one month we had sold the Wood Street house, and in two, as jaunty as a family in an early 1960s comedy, we had packed up all the chapter books, and baseball cards (bought and sold like stocks), and paper bags of torn children-drawn masterpieces, and old Easter baskets dribbling static fake hay. We poured the heaps in our closets into boxes and swept in the bureau tops of kiln-fired blobs for good measure. We hired a small U-Haul a week before the official moving day because we couldn't wait to get started. And with the wedding china in my lap and some of our slightly broken junk antiques breaking slightly more in the back, we rattled up the hill, stepping out like Christopher Columbuses on the muddy precipice of our new world.

BY THE TIME we moved to Nashawtuc Hill, the real estate agents in town had begun calling the woodsy section on its backside also Nashawtuc Hill, despite the fact it was utterly flat. New houses had been cropping up there for years, but none was as splendid as the pillared mansion one handsome young couple from the Midwest had built there several years earlier, with a groomed acre stretching out in the front and tiny yard behind and a perfect living room as untouched by human habitation as Thoreau's Maine woods. It was a fairyland of white carpet and pale silky curtains and matching sofas and glistening, virginal fireplace utensils and large treated-silver-framed photographs of beautiful horseback-riding daughters atop a brand-new baby grand. No one I knew had ever set foot on this sacred ground, except, presumably, the owners helicoptered in once a year for the family Christmas card picture. Man, woman, and child were routed into the house through the capacious mudroom entrance, which funneled one off to the enormous, gorgeous kitchen, a land sufficient unto itself. "What do you have to do to get into that living room?" queried a friend who had finally accepted an invitation to a cocktail party in order to do so, only to be clapped on the back and ushered past the teeming throng down into the basement with the mahogany bar.

Until I moved back to Concord, I had never known anyone who lived in such a house. Suddenly it seemed as if half the boys Hunter and Teddy played with lived in the enormous houses that had popped up in developments all over the Concord and West Concord farmlands. The farmers' daughters who had been my childhood friends had lived without luxury in stark, paint-peeling Victorian houses too close to the road. But by the 1990s, many of these farmers had become millionaires, selling off their farms to developers who plowed every last twig or tree or barn or wildflower field under, covering the land with sprayed-on grass and fuss-pot bushes surrounded by cedar chips and giant bold houses built cheek to cheek. Whenever you turned at a road sign that had "Farm" in the title, you were never sure what you might find—a house that looked like a function center or a small castle or a Mediterranean villa, but the one thing you knew you wouldn't find was a farm.

But the houses—if only my Puritan God had allowed me to live in one! The people who graced them came from everywhere but New England and were blissfully unaware of its shabby-genteel mandates: houses must be a hundred years or older, with clanking underused furnaces and a single window-unit air conditioner not to be retrieved from the attic until a heat wave rendered it a punishment to carry down; living rooms must be furnished with a motley of hand-me-down armchairs and sofas, slept on by large dirty dogs; rooms not in direct use must be shut off and unheated. Whereas the owners of the new houses actually seemed to enjoy living in them. And why not? For these houses were light and endlessly spacious, with gymnasium-size kitchens and lavish media rooms, and living rooms whose beautifully coordinated furniture had been bought by a decorator, and vaulted skylit hallways where the sun hit your face like a searchlight, and glass kitchen walls overlooking turquoise pools. They were the Disney version of *The Philadelphia Story*, with grand stairways and oak-paneled libraries. I didn't want to like these houses—forgive me, Lord, for I have sinned—but what was not to like? No wonder the mothers and fathers in them beamed, as if thanking their lucky stars to be there, so happy to see you when you trudged in reluctantly in twelve-hour-old makeup to pick up your kids. Graciously they greeted you in their Versailles foyer, ushering you in to take a home-made brownie on the gleaming plate on the gleaming granite counter that slid endlessly around the baked-on-painted, curving-cabineted kitchen. The fathers bouncing forward in expensive new gym clothes, the mothers a little worn but pretty, perfectly made up, like aging country western singers, with long wavy coiffed hair and a trace of Southern accent. They had wanted these houses with no trees between them, a ready-made neighborhood to live in for a few years until the husbands rose in the company and they moved again.

And if these parents did not appreciate the charm of the large crack in my front door, they were not alone. My children's faces had dropped too at the sight of the old linoleum and dirty carpeting and 1960s bathrooms of our recent purchase on Nashawtuc Hill. And my heart had been pierced when our insurance appraiser walking through the house had said in a worried voice, "So how's Charlie's business doing?" And I'd suffered a pang when I heard the carpenters who had worked on our first house openly debating whether the house was a move down, as if they were as invested in our standing as we, and I had not kept up my end.

But though the tradesmen and my children thought we'd gone down in the world, my parents thought we'd gone up. Every few days my mother would arrive with a flutter to drop a clipping or book on my kitchen table, entering my house, like the Indians of old, and just as annoyingly, without knocking. The truth was, I wasn't so happy to see her anymore, for as my parents had become rich, we were rapidly going broke. Just as we'd moved to Nashawtuc Hill, Charlie's documentary film work had dried up. With sinking heart every morning, I would watch him climb a ladder to paint the trim or wash the windows. We'd had no income for a year. And slowly but surely shame and mortification had begun to settle on my soul.

And yet up there on the hilltop that first summer and fall, with the air so breezy, with the river glinting below and the traffic on Elm Street a distant rumble, with the old screen door on the old shingled porch slamming so comfortingly behind us, Charlie and I could not help but still believe in our own fantasy. Though the bank owned the house and we owed the bank, though Charlie's phone machine at work was always blinking zero, though my parents' increased worth had only added to their anxious penury, nevertheless Charlie would waltz over from his office over the garage for lunch and sit out on the stone terrace and sigh, saying he knew he should be worried but somehow sitting there, out over the hill, the very hill where the for-

midable sachem had once guarded her people, he just could
not help but think all was well.

How could we not be at peace? For next to us, in a very
large house on six acres, lived the Alfords, he who had
grown up on the hill and brought his family back in middle
age, offering us the use of their old tennis court the first
time we met them; they were unassuming, amiable, unen-
croaching neighbors, so embarrassed by the grandeur of
their kitchen, they were spending thousands to reduce its
size. And below us, in an Acorn prefab house lived no-
nonsense Hal Bradford, a lean, good-looking man of inde-
terminate age, out tending his large vegetable garden at ten
on a Monday morning, or putting up a water conservation
notice, or raking and pruning the conservation trails. A
mild, pleasant, gently moralizing Yankee, Hal had given
millions of dollars' worth of his family's land to the town
without affixing its name to any of it. Hal was a man with
deep pockets but modest needs; a man of strong but silent
demeanor, who would appear like magic whenever someone so much as lifted an ax to shrub in the town's protected
wetlands. When Hunter broke a window in Hal Bradford's
old half-falling-down shed, Hunter had come running up
the hill upset, confused, guilty, and a little indignant because Hal had suggested that Hunter, who had never even

made his own bed, might work off the damages by doing a few chores.

And then there was the pine-needled tramp of dog-walking women in shapeless, comfortable clothes and mannish boots relentlessly padding past Charlie's office window every morning and afternoon. "And you wonder why we're still married," Charlie would cry out, gesturing wildly, as a particularly shabbily layered crew passed. "Look at the competition!" But I had joined the competition, though I was one of the younger of the dog-women living on Nashawtuc Hill at that time; my only friend was Kay, a red-haired, no-makeup beauty from old non–New England money who had embraced ancient-station-wagon New England ways with the zeal of a convert. Kay had a penchant for ladies clubs; in a gathering she could be found basking in the wintry warmth of the briskest old girl there. Kay had the most beautiful house in the neighborhood—one gasped in her front hall to see the wide river sweeping below you—but in twenty-five years living there, Kay had left her Formica kitchen untouched by the tomfoolery of $10,000 stoves and $5,000 refrigerators.

Then one bone-chilling day out walking around Nashawtuc Hill, I heard a new homeowner utter an historic phrase, never before uttered in the town of Concord, Massachusetts: "Money is no object."

CHAPTER TWELVE

TRANSCENDENTAL REAL ESTATE

THE CONCORD TRANSCENDENTALISTS were always per-
fecting their homes—adding on, starting over, moving up.
They were as heady with rebellion from their rigid, Calvinistic parents as my contemporaries and I were from our
own Depression-era parents. They believed they were not

---

*The Wayside, formerly Hillside, has been owned by three
Concord authors: Bronson Alcott, Nathaniel Hawthorne, and
Margaret Sidney—author of* The Five Little Peppers and
How They Grew—*who I thought was by far the
most famous, until I grew up.*

predestined, that they could improve themselves and their lives, that hope sprang eternal. Whenever I stand in one of Emerson's, Hawthorne's, Thoreau's, or the Alcotts' houses, I feel the same high I always feel whenever a carpenter rips into a wall with a saw.

And so, as much as I delight in hating Bronson Alcott, the sad truth is, when it comes to houses and the deeply shallow joy we take from them—we are one. Despite his sanctimonious outcry against private ownership, it was real estate that saved Bronson. Suicidal after the dissolution of Fruitlands, he cheered right up when he became a homeowner, becoming addicted to the best antidepressant known to middle-aged man and woman: fixing up your house.

At first, of course, Bronson would have "nothing to do with" such a non-utopian venture as the purchase of Hillside. "I will not abide in a house set aside for myself and family alone," he said loftily, though apparently he made no fuss on moving day. The disintegrating, pre-Revolutionary house—a low-ceilinged, four-room dwelling with a yard dotted with pig-rooting holes—would have reduced my parents to tears. But Bronson was energized. He christened the sorry pig farm "Hillside" and joyfully attacked it with ambition and artistry, dragging over sheds to enlarge the house and moving plants around the yard. And when he

needed a break, he found a captive audience in Henry Thoreau, who, unlike the less and less available Emerson, had
little choice but to be home when Bronson called—it
was probably from Hillside Thoreau had borrowed the
ax in 1845 to construct his own antidepressant, the cabin
at Walden Pond. Meanwhile, Marmee was pulling out her
hair over life's (and real estate's) biggest qualifier: money.
(Bronson's only suggestion was: Why didn't they build a
cabin at the pond?) Though it might have been nice to see
a smile on Bronson's face again, serenity and the odd apple
did not feed three teenagers and an eight-year-old. Marmee, who had hoped at Hillside to be alone at last with her
immediate family, had to open her small house to boarders, and also take on the full-time care of a mentally chal-
lenged girl.

But at least at Hillside, Louisa got the room of her own
that she longed for, a bedroom provided by Marmee, filled
with aromatic herbs and a door that opened to the woods,
a place where she could write. "Write poetry," her mother
had advised as therapy for her adolescent angst. While my
parents and their friends had worried about praise going to
their children's heads, Marmee had been more like the parents in my generation who are so obsessed with building
confidence regardless of merit, their progeny have been
criticized as being too confident. Louisa could never be too

confident, thanks to her hypercritical father, but thanks to her mother, who applauded her every little attempt, she learned to believe in her writing. My parents were too nervous to enjoy anything I wrote until their friends approved it. "Frankly we were a bit underwhelmed when we first read this," my father said after rereading an essay after it had run word for word in *The New York Times*, "but now we love it." And, yet—how can I blame them, since half of what I wrote was based on them? When I was asked to read a piece (in which my mother was an "amusing character") at my mother's club as a fun surprise, I'd accepted with sinking heart, knowing that the surprise would not be fun.

The petty earnings of the Alcott women could not pay the bills. Some two years in, the only way Hillside could save the Alcotts was for them to sell it so they could eat. The problem was, nobody would buy it. It had fallen into disrepair again—clearly Bronson's improvements had been on the flimsy side, as ephemeral as all his work.

Desperate, Marmee abandoned Hillside, unsold, to take a full-time job in Boston, moving her family to a basement apartment with no parlor. In Boston, the Alcotts moved around to various awful apartments, got sick, and, except for Bronson, worked too hard for too little at jobs they didn't like. "The pathetic family" (as Louisa took to calling it) returned to Concord ten years after leaving it, just in time for Beth to expire in a rented room. Louisa had been fantasizing about dying herself ever since she was a preteen and her father was tossing the coin between celibacy and free love. But it was Beth who got to die.

Meanwhile, Bronson blissfully threw himself into fixing up another crumbling Concord dwelling bought with his wife's money, Orchard House.

CHAPTER THIRTEEN

MONEY IN A SMALL TOWN

"WHATEVER YOU DO, you are not to talk to the children about money," Charlie said to me with great wisdom many years ago. But even if I had wanted to talk to the children about money, what could I have said? The more I delve into the matter, the more confused and mortifying the feelings become.

Concord has always been a haven for people screwed up

Marmee would scurry down the Concord streets
in fear of shopkeepers.

about money. The countless progeny of the Puritan Reverend Bulkeley—who'd arrived in Concord with six thousand pounds sterling—might not have been too delighted that he had given away most of his money when he died, but I'm sure he was. The anxiety that Puritanism produced about money still shakes my hometown. By the time I was growing up, moralistic conflict about money had pretty much taken the place of religion. I don't remember if my parents ever used God in a sentence when I was little, but I certainly heard plenty about the value of a dollar on the one hand, and money as the root of all evil on the other. As a result, when it comes to money, I don't know whether I'm coming or going (well, clearly, I'm going, like most New Englanders who own a framed genealogy of the family but no longer the Copley portrait). I don't know whether I want people to think I'm rich or I'm poor; frugal, extravagant, or generous. I feel miserable when I spend money and sad when I don't.

When it comes to money, the New England Protestant treads cautiously, as if God is watching. When a Concord friend assures me proudly that she will be buying my new book, but "only when it comes out in paperback," I am supposed to be as proud of her as the God she is so shamelessly courting. Frugality as a divine virtue was even more pervasive back in Emerson and Thoreau's time, when so many were dying young and God was a part of everyday conversation. The New England reformers were just trying to get out from under a Protestantism that crushed them, but not even Thoreau could escape the morass Protestantism presented about money. Thoreau may have been deeply radical for his time (*A snowstorm is more to me than Christ,* he said on his deathbed). But for someone who wished to be above money, Thoreau was obsessively meticulous, paying his father his rent to the halfpenny and devoting the opening chapter of *Walden* to an exact accounting of each nail purchased. Only Emerson seemed to have escaped the Protestant angst about money.

When Charlie and I lived beyond our means in Concord, it was with a desperate bravado. But one of the great things about Emerson was how graciously he lived beyond his. Though he had grown up in the basement of his widowed mother's boardinghouse with four brothers and one coat to share, when he bought his first house, moving to Concord with his second wife, it was grand enough to have been called "the castle." Soon he was handing out large sums of money to Bronson Alcott, and hosting the flirty, high-maintenance Margaret Fuller and the supercilious Thoreau, all from that New England rarity—unqualified generosity.

Emerson was directly descended from the self-sacrificing Peter Bulkeley, in a line of New England ministers so somber their only relief had been in dying young. His overly critical father had griped that his son, not yet three, "doesn't read very well." Emerson's influential aunt, the famously disagreeable Mary Moody Emerson, though "not a Calvinist wished everyone else to be one." But Emerson was no self-loathing New Englander conflicted about money.

The most astonishing example of this was the bravery (or unscrewed-up-ness) it took for Emerson to go after the money of his dead first wife—the poetic teenager Ellen Tucker. Even marrying her took courage, for when the twenty-five-year-old Emerson met the beautiful, rich sixteen-year-old, she was glowing feverishly with the TB that had already killed a father and brother, and soon would take her mother and sister. The marriage was deliriously happy, and when Ellen died at age twenty, the deranged Emerson walked daily to her grave in a neighboring town for six months (until he opened up her coffin and looked inside). And yet he had the presence of mind to sue her family for the fortune that would allow him the latitude to lead his generous life. "How mercenary!" one from New England is tempted to cry out, for in New England mentioning, and in some cases, even *knowing* the terms of a will is considered vulgar. Six months after my mother was left money, jewelry, and furniture by her rich aunt, she still had no idea how much or what she had inherited and asked that the furniture be auctioned off sight unseen. Even I, who think of nothing but money and have actually *inherited* money, would not dream of asking to read a will. But Emerson did not have my hang-ups. He checked first with Ellen's dying mother and sister to see if they needed the money (they didn't), and then took the greedy brother-in-law who wouldn't relinquish Ellen's money to the courts. I couldn't have done it, not after less than two years of marriage. I would have been too obsessed with appearances— but then I am not the man Emerson was.

I am—when it comes to money—more like the man Hawthorne was: a mess.

The Hawthornes would never forget the three years they lived in Concord by the river. Arriving at The Old Manse from their wedding, they'd found a vegetable garden planted by Thoreau. Their first child (a daughter) had been born there, and Hawthorne had written his melancholy stories happily and published them to acclaim. The problem was, Hawthorne hadn't been paid what he was owed and he had left Concord broke, forced to move back into his reclusive mother's house in Salem. But instead of blaming his publishers for his poverty, he'd blamed himself, writing later of his "ill-success in life": "I am ashamed of it, and I ought to be."

MONEY AND ONE'S ATTITUDE TOWARD IT is so intrinsic to the New Englander's identity that it is nearly impossible for him or her to have objectivity toward it. As moths to the flame, old-moneyed Yankees are drawn to bemoaning their lack of money even in front of, say, the person who cleans their house. Having money was nobody's business, in this complicated culture, but *not* having it (as long, of course, as you actually *did* have it)—was a subject suitable for any audience. Somehow as a child I knew that my parents' friends, the Forresters—who lived in a magnificent house and sent each child to private school—had told one posh school that they simply couldn't afford the tuition that year. The school was so embarrassed, being old-moneyed itself, it allowed the Forrester child to attend for free, without ever checking out the Forrester bank account.

Her own suicide attempt, her breakdown, her children's breakdowns—these, my mother could cheerily sanction me writing about. Even about sex, as long as it wasn't graphic, my mother could abide. (Though not my father, who, underlining a sentence about going to third base in the manuscript of my first novel, had written pointedly in the margins, "I wasn't born yesterday.") But about money I could not write. Money was the taboo, never to be mentioned, except in terms of the lack of it. We were supposed to be above money growing up, and yet we were always thinking of it: real butter and ice cream limited to Sunday, as if earned after the grind of church; allowances deducted from, motels without TVs, secondhand instruments bought for music lessons, a two new-outfit limit for school each fall. In fairness, my parents had had to be on a tight budget when I was little: it was not the frugality but the attitude behind it that confused me, because the parents of my friends who lived in modest houses in the wrong part of town and seemed to have less money, seemed far less concerned about it, giving lavish gifts at Christmas and birthdays and new clothes out of the blue. But these parents, unlike my parents and their friends, had not come from money.

My parents' friends either had money or, like my mother, had come from money. They would talk about their lack of it, either because they didn't want people to know they had it, or because, having once had it, they actually felt poor. "Oh, they have heaps of money," was constantly being said about somebody by my parents, even, in my parents' last years, after they could be said to have heaps of money themselves. On the way to a restaurant, I would be mortified to hear them calculating whether they owed someone dinner and should pick up the check (though frankly, who has not done this, at least mentally). How much each person was due was weighed with the precision of a fine jeweler. It was impossible not to believe that money was love.

When I became a mother, I didn't want anyone to think I was counting. If a child's friend came along to a child's haircut, I treated the friend; off to the movies I went spur of the moment with a group of kids for a quick eighty bucks; I sent so many nervous little packets of gifts to Emily and her friend at overnight camp, the camp had to institute a rule against parental packages. I was afraid that my children wouldn't feel loved; that the little tyke trying to hand me money her mother had given her for the games at the bowling alley—wouldn't feel loved; that the postman at Christmas wouldn't feel loved; that the guy who came to clean the stair carpet (to whom I gave a 50 percent tip) wouldn't feel loved; that the guests sitting down to way too much food at Thanksgiving—wouldn't feel loved.

How could I deny my children the new skis and fancy sneakers and expensive camps that my parents had denied me, when the credit companies were so gracious? Long ago, in the early years of motherhood, I had felt so guilty that I only paid the tiny minimum on my credit card every month, I'd been terrified to open a letter from the credit card company—only to find myself congratulated on being such a good customer and handsomely rewarded with a higher limit. One year, everyone got a lovely red-boxed gift from Saks Fifth Avenue because it was the only card that worked. When I dashed off to the grocery store and called out to Charlie, "Should I use the MasterCard?" I would hear gaily shouted back, "Well, you can always give it a try!"

We spent money as if we had no choice, my head throbbing and Charlie's back spasming with guilt. Once I had suggested it might help if I wrote out the checks, only to have Charlie toss me a pile of bills with the instruction, "Just pay half." Even after a good year producing his documentary films, Charlie had never known what the next year would bring. His back was out for weeks at a time. "It's like having a member of the homeless in my own house," I had cried out as he lay for a third day in the TV room with a milk carton beside him, even the dogs refusing to enter. Then Charlie learned the trick of expressing his negative feelings, which I had been so insistent upon teaching the boys. "I hate you *and* I love you!" four-year-old Teddy had cried out, to my "Good for you!" and Charlie's "I can't take this!" as he fled the scene. But now Charlie might say blithely, "We're going under," as he gently drifted off to a deep sleep, leaving me frozen awake the rest of the night.

When Charlie's work dried up that first year on Nashaw-tuc Hill, we bought all our food on credit, but we still took the kids on a winter vacation because we didn't want them to know we couldn't afford it. And when the impossible bills came in, we punished ourselves and each other. "I can never say no to you!" Charlie said, but it was a failing of his I found impossible to abhor. The answer had always been *No* growing up, and when we filled up the cart at Toys "Я" Us a mile high and crossed our fingers on the credit card, I turned to Charlie and said, tears in my eyes, "I love you so much!"

OF COURSE, it would have been extremely helpful if my "work," about which I was so serious, had produced anything approximating a salary. But by the time we moved to Nashawtuc Hill, I felt as helpless about earning money as my mother had.

"I've always said Sally will make more money than I," Charlie had been fond of saying back in the beginning of my writing career. The Social Security Administration informed me a handful of years ago that I had made, to date, an average annual salary of $5,000. Now, as I descend from the podium to the applause of whatever crowd I have been asked (gratis) to address—high school kids, retirees, a bookstore where there is only one person in the audience, and that person is my husband—my hair freshly dyed, my expensive suit (bought exclusively for speaking engagements) professionally cleaned, Charlie says, "You are the most successful failure I know." Meaning that it seems actually to cost me to write. At least Thoreau—who used his own money to print a thousand copies of his first book and then had to haul seven hundred unsold copies back to his mother's house because his publisher couldn't even be bothered to store them—didn't have dry cleaning bills.

In Concord, there were the working mothers and the at-home full-time mothers, and then there was me, longing to belong, but, as usual, not sure to which group. The two groups were much divided, though not along financial lines. (A Rothschild might work full time as a doctor; a plumber's wife might stay home.) Everyone was guilty about either working or not working, but the working mothers, deeply grateful to those taking up the collection for the soccer coach presents, were friendlier to the full-time mothers than the other way around. This was particularly true in the preschool years. Interviewing for an open slot for Emily in the town's most popular cooperative, I'd been informed by the parent volunteer that every set of parents was required to clean the school one Saturday a month. "Couldn't parents just hire a cleaner for the school instead of leaving the kids at home with a babysitter?" I'd asked. "We feel," said the volunteer, "that it's important that the mothers and fathers do the actual cleaning." I'd also been informed that parents were required to parent-help one morning every two weeks, no babysitters allowed. "Well," I'd huffed as I pulled Emily from the school roster, "I guess you discriminate against working mothers."

But was I a working mother? You would think so, to watch the breezy certitude with which I declined the community duties the full-time mothers took on. No, no, I was sorry but I could not attend anything before the hour of two-thirty, because I was *working*. Even my poor children, sick with flu, were required to throw up from a mattress dragged into my office while the genius was at work. There were no exceptions, except for—real estate. Charlie would look out his office window, perplexed to see me at eleven a.m. rushing off in some near-stranger's car dressed to the nines. "Cissey Collins is looking at that Colonial on Garfield!" I'd explain with a shout as we whizzed away.

As for the working mothers—many of them seemed to have interesting jobs, but I never learned the details, because I was too busy bragging about the latest casting changes in the movie of my first novel. Julia Roberts and Kiefer Sutherland! Winona Ryder and Johnny Depp! I updated people in the coffee line at Coggins Bakery. "So, how's the movie going?" my new friend behind the counter would ask, and coaxed out of my shell, I would spew forth. Then—mercifully for everyone but me—the option expired on my movie deal.

"Just think if you wrote a book about something people actually wanted to read about . . ." Charlie mused more than once. Not perhaps a nonfiction book about the family poet from a writer who admits on page one that she doesn't get poetry (my third book). And might not I have written at least one tiny little sex scene in my second novel, as my editor had begged—not a lot to ask from a comic romance about a marriage breakup? ("I thought you were writing the *big* book," Charlie had said when I'd told him the subject.) But WASPs cannot write convincingly about sex, yet another reason for the group's decline in the arts. Anything I tried came out as cheap and unsexy as poor old Edith Wharton's foray in the field, as found in the appendix of her 1990s biography. A friend of my mother's had been sent the biography by her own mother with the appendix neatly excised. "I'm sixty years old!" my mother's friend had cried out when the new book had arrived, mangled.

The truth is, my writing has been less a real job than a punishing luxury. After all my efforts to be different from my mother and her friends, I, like them, have not worked for the money. Recently, yet another insurance agent made the usual annoying assumption while chatting me up in my living room at ten a.m., saying, "So, you work in the home?" But this time, I didn't reply with my usual "No, no, I'm a writer," followed by, "Oh, do I know any of your books?" followed by, "No, no, *nobody* reads my books." I simply said, "Yes."

AND YET I HAD BEEN so determined to be a working mother, so contemptuous of my own mother as a housewife. Her primary functions, in my jaded teen eyes, seemed to be laying out the can of dog food and the dog bowl and the can opener for one of her children to feed Scout, and folding our clean clothes into designated baskets for us to carry chorefully to our rooms. I'd seen the crises of her daily life and thought, *Well, if I'm going to be a wreck over what to serve on the Fourth of July, I might as well be a wreck over a career.* Still, if I'd had to choose between being a full-time professional outside the home or a full-time housewife, I would have had to choose the latter, I realize now. As it turned out, I needed to be home when my kids came home from school, more, I suppose, than anything else.

I was obsessive, as obsessively driven to make my house cozy as I had once been driven to find a man. I *had* to make a fire before supper in the winter, I *had* to shop all day

Saturday so I could deliver the same four healthy meals in rotation during the week. "Oh, no," Teddy cried out recently, heading out the door as I began cooking something from a magazine, "I'm leaving and you're actually making something different!" To avoid the kind of bickering that had punctuated my childhood dinners, I had assigned no chores. "Go ahead and start without me!" I called out as the children came to my prettily laid table, on the theory they had tons of homework. I once calculated that I put in at least twenty-five hours per week (shopping, and cooking, and doing the dishes), so my teenage boys could say gruffly, as I finally sat down to join them, "Thanks for dinner, Mom," as they rose from the table.

So much of it was worthless: as when I sweated for two days to get the house ready for five-year-old Emily's birthday party. Surely none of her friends noticed, let alone cared, that the stairway carpet had been freshly vacuumed. And some of it might have been worse than worthless. "I know you hate doing all this," eleven-year-old Emily cries out—as I am panicking about a Christmas dinner for twenty-three, polishing silver bowls for chocolates and ironing the old linen napkins—"but I love it so much!" For Emily may have to waste countless hours one day to make it beautiful too.

But I had to be home. I had no choice. As the cruelest

of teenagers, eating my cinnamon toast after school while my mother puttered around in slippers nearby, though not *too* nearby, I had called out, "Stop shuffling!" But the truth was, I'd been glad—even then, *especially* then—so glad that my mother was home.

CHAPTER FOURTEEN

MRS. EMERSON AND MRS. PAYNE AND MRS. STUART

LOOKING BACK, through the mellowing detachment that has descended upon me, it is hard to grasp why my domestic duties as a mother should have filled me with so much angst. It is nice to think that I was desperate to create a kind of utopian childhood for my children. But it is hard

---

Emerson brought the world to his table, but it was his melancholic wife who worried about what would be served upon it.

not to believe that I was at least equally driven by the hope of an approving word. For when anyone came to my door— the random neighbor, Twinky Warren with yet another petition to sign, the former babysitter, the other mothers, the census taker, the storm-window guy, my parents' friends, my parents—I felt queasy with fear, waiting to be judged by the state of my house. "There's nothing I hate more than a messy sink," my mother said once. It is a statement that still guides me through my every day.

And yet, even more than I, my mother feared moral judgment on the state of her house—yet another legacy passed down from the fierce but frightened New England women who came before. Part of the Puritan creed had been that every activity, even the most minor domestic drudgery, should be carried out in grand piety of those who knew they were God's Chosen, so that even the state of one's bureau drawers was under the keen eye of Him. This is why my mother and her friends cleaned the house before the weekly cleaning lady came. And why even a woman with full-time servants, like Emerson's second wife, Lidian, could be paralyzed with fear about running her house. Emerson may have brought the world to his table, but it was the melancholic Lidian who worried herself, sometimes into a deep depression, about what would be served upon it.

LIDIAN WAS RIGHT to fear judgment on her domestic practices. When Emerson urged the half-starved Alcotts to move in after they moved to Concord, Bronson, ever the mooch, was all for it. Emerson, who refused to join Fruitlands and another nearby commune, Brook Farm, had the mad dream of other families living communally at his house at his expense. But Marmee had refused, very probably because she virulently disapproved of Lidian's household regime. So much so that when five-year-old Waldo Emerson died, Marmee couldn't bring herself to write Lidian a condolence letter. "I cannot offer sympathy to these dear suffering Mothers,— for I see so much culpable neglect of the means of living," Marmee wrote. Marmee was so obsessed with being good herself, she sometimes forgot to be kind. (Still, perhaps *no* condolence note was better than the one Thoreau wrote: "Do not the flowers die every autumn? He had not even taken root here. I was not startled to hear that he was dead. . . . It would have been strange if he had lived.")

But Lidian—brought up among "the religious terrors" of a chilly Calvinist family—was unkind only to herself. No amount of husbandly assistance—for even the aloof Emerson saw her suffering—could lift the overwhelming concept engulfing Lidian that she would be found wanting on even the smallest household endeavor. When her mother-in-law, who lived with them, mentioned once that she was bit tired of being served lamb—it was a criticism that Lidian "never forgot." About domestic matters her eldest daughter said of her mother: "It was her nature to take them with a curiously exaggerated view of their importance and to expend on them an amazing amount of indignation and shame."

When I read about Lidian Emerson, I know I am a Protestant, or more exactly, the daughter of a Protestant. When I think of Lidian, I think of my mother stoically moving through her daily life with her aching feet and head and stomach, clutched with fear over—nothing. I see her harrowed face the night before Thanksgiving thinking, *What if I forget to put the turkey in the oven or forget to take it out?* All through December my mother, while staunchly maintaining that she loves Christmas, is crushed by guilt and worry: *Should she give the hairdresser a nice bottle of sparkling wine, or does she really just want money? If she takes her daughter to the theater, should she compensate her sons? And when will she ever find the time to make the tiny jars of homemade eggnog she gives each year to her friends?*

"Every day another dream dies!" she would cry out over the phone all through December.

I had not known the depth of my mother's Puritan guilt until I moved back to Concord. Guilt from which she could only find relief on a trip, away from the grind of the daily domestic expectations. Nothing, nothing could beat a trip for my mother—down the Rhine, down the Tigris, down the Nile, my parents floated merrily, a target for terrorists in their white golfing hats and yellow-bright, perfectly pressed, spanking spring clothes. It didn't matter that my mother had been depressed for two months straight, crying all day long; it didn't matter that her feet hurt her so much she could barely walk. Out came the shot of cortisone and the Wash'n Wears. Traveling was the magic bullet that sent whole villages of my mother's guilts running for the hills.

Likewise, Lidian's misery was so acute—and you can only imagine what those unpaid bills did to her—that Emerson finally resorted to turning his house into a boarding-house and hiring someone else to run it, the theory being that he and his family would be paying boarders in their own home. It was an expensive venture and one that failed. Not until many years later, when Emerson was in his seventies and his own mental powers were failing with dementia and his eldest daughter was in full charge, did Lidian become a happy person. Quite simply, she no longer felt a duty to her husband to be a perfect housekeeper. Despite all his sympathy and generosity, there was at least one Protestant fault that Emerson had not escaped—the sin of believing that honesty was always a virtue. "She's *very* direct," a New Englander often says of another, as if it were a compliment. In his essay "Love," Emerson wrote effusively of the "mutual joy" a married couple finds in pointing out ("without offense") "the blemishes and hindrances in each other." If this be the joy of a long marriage, then I am overjoyed to have escaped it thus far. Surely part of Lidian's domestic torture was the fear of such affectionate criticisms from her husband. So when Emerson drifted into a sweet senility, Lidian became "a belle"—off to parties and lectures almost every night, positively glowing, like my mother on a trip.

CHAPTER FIFTEEN

GOD AND MIDDLE SCHOOL

IF YOU ARE A PURITAN, there is something warm and fuzzy about the thought of a punishing God. Once, after one of my sons' raucous middle school sleepovers, I'd found among the wreckage of pizza boxes and girlie magazines, a little pile of Berenstain Bear books, which had been sneaked in from Emily's room and hidden under one miscreant's grimy

---

The Old North Bridge, behind the Old Manse,
where Emerson's grandparents likely watched the
American Revolution commence.

pillow. Some Protestant adolescent—shocked by the sinful nature he'd discovered in himself—had lulled himself to sleep with the comfort of a guilt-tripping mama.

Hunter, as eldest, was the most Puritan of my children. He was in the fifth grade when we moved to Nashawtuc Hill and was still the same careful, hardworking, literal-minded boy who at age eight had accepted the nonexistence of Santa Claus from his mother's PC lips with a sober finality, without making the lateral leap of his younger brother. ("So I guess that's it for the Easter Bunny and the Tooth Fairy and Santa's little helpers.") In the fifth grade, Hunter, dying of tedium but resolute as his *Mayflower* forebears, had written a lengthy, comprehensive report on the father of the polio vaccine ("In 1925 Jonas Salk enters junior high," read a sentence of his 100-line summary), while Teddy had dashed off time-is-running-out inspired book reports on the bus, surprising himself with the power of his own last-ditch conclusions. Hunter, in the fifth grade, still worried that he would hurt the waiter's feelings if he didn't clean his plate. Hunter was so good and true, I secretly feared he would become a nerd.

Then Hunter entered middle school.

In mid–sixth grade, the screws loosen in Hunter's teenaging brain. And Hunter, once so reliable, at age thirteen forgets he has left his little sister in the garage unattended.

To the immense shock of his mother, Hunter raises the flame of a Bic lighter to the ceiling of his room before an audience of admiring peers and is grounded for the week-end. His brother, filled with unexplained joy, rises that Saturday to clean up his room unsolicited, murmuring, "I just don't know why I am so happy." In the seventh grade, Hunter buzzes off his bowl cut as if bound for the electric chair; in eighth grade, he is escorted home at two a.m. by police. Caught skateboarding off the library steps, Hunter is severely reprimanded by a gaggle of librarians, while Teddy earns that rarity—collective librarian laughter—with his, "I guess we'll just have to go do drugs." Hunter is always caught, his transgressions performed in the sight of God, while Teddy, with a dozen more infractions, slips away, or charms away.

In elementary school, Teddy had been class clown and class delight, the teachers' (and everyone else's) secret boy-friend. In the fifth grade, he had soared at schoolwork and shined up the house with his good humor, hanging around me so much I had privately called him Piece of Tape. One night Charlie and I had even invited Teddy along on our weekly date, and Teddy had sat between us at the movies, as one. Then Teddy entered middle school. "How fast was the decline . . ." Teddy said recently when his sixth-grade report card surfaced. By December, the bright spot in the class is now the class disrupter, verging on delinquent. Returning home from sixth-grade detention one cold afternoon, Teddy brandishes his perfectly punctuated, deeply sarcastic penance for the music teacher, Ms. Plotz: "I'm sorry I said 'helk' in music class. I should never have said 'helk' in class. I promise never, ever, to say 'helk' again." After several sleepless nights, I discover Teddy whistling off to school with a plastic bag of sugar labeled "cocaine"—for a skit for music, I am informed blithely, Ms. Plotz having discovered Teddy plays guitar.

IN THE CONCORD middle school just as the adolescent started searching for his new identity, his old identity, so lovingly nurtured in elementary school, was snatched away. In middle school, each hour meant a different teacher, a teacher who might remember a child's name, but not his parents' and his little sister's and his dog's. In middle school, the children were transported to a school far away from their elementary school, away from Ms. Groe from first grade who might have waved to her former charges as they turned adolescent—reminding them of Valentine's Day when everyone was assured a valentine from everyone else; reminding them that Teddy the skateboarder had once been Teddy the teacher's star helper when it came to writing the date on the board; reminding them how good it felt to be good.

My brothers and I had also changed teachers every hour in junior high, but we'd been more prepared—toughened by strict elementary school teachers wielding letter grades and parents never summoned except for dire delinquency. In my kids' elementary school, there'd been enough positive reinforcement from smiling in-class mothers and teachers to satisfy the most worried Puritan child. "A strength!" Hunter and Teddy and 99 percent of their classmates had scored in all ten thousand redundant categories on their un-letter-graded elementary school report cards: "Cooperates with peers—a strength!" "Works well with others—a strength!" Elementary students, considered equally talented, had alternated leads in the school play, changing parts so often that the parents in the audience had had to relinquish all hope of understanding what the plays were about. In middle school, this nurturing delusion of noncompetitive achieving was abruptly terminated. Letter grades were introduced—the C replacing "Age Appropriate," proving that despite all the preaching of egalitarianism, being average was not pretty; while the D, replacing "Needs Improvement," shouted that the child would never get into college.

In middle school the hallways were as fraught as the

George Washington Bridge on a Friday afternoon, with kids merging from three elementary schools—kids, suddenly uncertain of who they were, desperate to prove themselves at any expense, but particularly the expense of one another. Select girls of low-to-middling academic standing, once lost in the crowd, now rode herd, their talent for bullying released into a large, unsupervised arena. A girl named Miranda, boasting a halo of golden curls but no angel, a little tough without the allure of the tramp, soared with a bravado that would eventually take her far, or take her down. Miranda wandered over to our house one afternoon with a pack of followers, to ask seven-year-old Emily, "Are you a lesbian?" to hoots of laughter. Miranda ran the middle school with her verbal policing skills, reducing Hunter, so cool in the eighth grade that even his teachers admitted it grudgingly, to tears one Tuesday night. Breaking rank, he came to my bedroom door at eleven p.m., pouring out in a rush: "Miranda says she won't be my friend unless I break up with my girlfriend!" *Who wants such a friend as Miranda*, I dared not say, for to malign Miranda was to blaspheme. I listened to Hunter, pierced to the soul with these ethical questions, and guided him to the solution of sticking to his girlfriend and telling Miranda she could do as she pleases. "What did Miranda say?" I asked the next afternoon when Hunter arrived home from school with a clear brow. Hunter shrugged, "Oh, she said, that's fine, she's still my friend, and now she's going out with Teddy."

Then came the heart-stopping day when Hunter was suspended from school for—sexual harassment! Hunter, who I had always worried was too moral. Hunter, who at nine had given his best friend his new $10 bill, saying, "He saved my life, Mom, that bureau was about to fall over on me." Then, after I'd explained in my life-lessons way that you didn't pay a friend for saving your life, he'd whispered, "But Mom, Jack's father has been out of work for a year!" Now with Hunter's suspension I had to try and understand the moral battle Hunter must have been waging. In middle school being cool wasn't counterproductive enough; Hunter must always be fighting the wrong battles for the right reasons. He'd been suspended, I'd finally gleaned, for calling a jeering girl who had written jeering letters to his depressive friend, "ugly," Hunter producing the incriminating letters for the school authorities only after the suspension was over, because he hadn't wanted to snitch, not even on the mean girl. Though a self-designated bad boy, he still had his moral standards. If only Hunter had grown up in the late 1960s when causes were handed you on a silver platter. But instead he said things like, "Mom, do you think it's fair that your insurance allows you to buy medicine so cheaply?"

Charlie and I had gone over to the middle school to endure the zero-tolerance palaver of Ms. Forbetta, the principal, in a hopeless attempt to get the suspension expunged. At Ms. Forbetta's suggestion, we gloomily dragged ourselves back to the middle school the next week for Parent-Teen Dialogue Night—as parents' penance for Hunter's suspension. It would be the first time Charlie and I had graced a parent-school-wide meeting since the year we had moved to Concord. Then, with delirious delusions of taking part in this democratic town still run by town meeting(!), we'd attended a PTA meeting and crawled out after three hours, wanting to put a gun to everyone's head including our own. ("What about AIDS?" a father had asked somberly early on, and Charlie had thought, *Wow, that's progressive, a discussion about AIDS in kindergarten!* only to find a twenty-minute discussion about teacher aides off and running.) In elementary school, I had parent-helped a maximum once-a-year; but in middle school, I had outdone my shirking self, never once setting foot in the building, as afraid of my sons now as I had once been of their friends' mothers. As a result, when we'd gone to see the principal after Hunter's suspension, we hadn't known which of the two overly dolled-up women sitting in the office was the principal.

Now I wondered if I should have gone to more school

functions and mother coffees. The mother coffees had always been held at one of the enormous houses in the treeless developments named after the obliterated farms—though today the trees have grown in and the real estate values fallen, the houses no longer new. The one coffee I had attended, I'd listened with head pounding to a woman with a 10,000-square-foot house, whose birth sons were named Chatterley and London and whose two adopted children had just been made American citizens! Now at Parent-Teen Dialogue Night I wondered if we should have gone to church for more than that one single year (when I'd caved to the kids). Not that "Christian" would have been the word to describe the family's reaction to getting up early on a Sunday morning and having to look nice.

As I looked around me at Parent-Teen Dialogue Night, my heart sank. I found myself thinking that none of the other kids looked as if they needed parent-teen dialogue at all, but like student council types who would breeze into college. When Hunter's best friend in fifth grade had been elected, I'd mentioned that maybe Hunter might want to get elected to student council one day, a suggestion even at that age greeted by derisive laughter.

And yet, as we were divided into groups and I was stuck with the articulate teen moderator who would, without a doubt, continue all through high school to rise at eight a.m.

every Saturday to "give back to the community" while my sons were nursing hangovers—I glimpsed, for a second, Hunter's point. For while these attractive, confident, a-little-too-good teens might one day lead the world, they bore no relation to Hunter as a teen, or me as a teen, or Charlie as a teen, or any of my friends as teens. And if identifying with a group is everything in adolescence, I couldn't be surprised that Hunter, in the group one table over, never opened his mouth once during the ensuing hour and a half of bright discussion. Hunter never spoke unless he had something to say, and clearly, in this crowd, he had nothing to say. And suddenly, for once, I too had nothing to say. For if these teen leaders were the Elect, how could I blame Hunter, in the either-or of middle school, for choosing to be on the side of the Damned?

CHAPTER SIXTEEN

REREADING
LITTLE WOMEN

EVERY TEN YEARS, when they were not putting on *The Night Thoreau Spent in Jail*, the Concord Players put on *Little Women*, the Concord matrons bringing an effusive maturity to the roles of the teenage girls. In my early twenties, when I had committed enough sins to make Marmee's

---

Orchard House, streaming with busloads of Japanese tourists and out-of-town retirees, the men with blank, mystified faces, wondering why they are here and when they get to eat again.

blood boil, my secret hope was that I would be called back to Concord from my crummy apartment across from Sears, Roebuck in Cambridge to play the tragic, angelic Beth. I was twenty-three. That year I had moved four times, had three low-level jobs, and three failed romances. The concept of being Beth on the creaky old stage on Walden Street and getting to wither away for hours, while the likes of Mr. Gap and Mrs. Beech (my parents' good friends) and Jake O'Reilly (my fifth-grade boyfriend) were hovering around me, had a sudden appeal. Unfortunately, when last seen in Concord, I'd been a brash eighteen-year-old in a shrinking sweater dress brandishing a cigarette down Thoreau Street. So though I was called by the Concord Players to audition for the slutty, adulteress girlfriend in *Witness for the Prosecution*, no one called me to play Beth.

The theory behind Beth in life and fiction was that she was simply too good to live. Beth was the middle child in a crush of spotlight grabbers: Marmee with her histrionics, Bronson with his sweeping saintliness, Louisa ("Jo") with her black moods and dreams of glory, and the spoiled baby, May ("Amy"), with her demands for luxuries. Even the bovine eldest, Anna ("Meg"), had the spirit to seek the full panoply of romantic love. But Beth asked only to stay home and sweep the floor.

That Beth was born to die for our sins has proved so

serviceable a concept that her expiration on the page, screen, and stage continues to evoke a cleansing shower from the eyes of even the most cynical female. Women's liberation is a fairly new phenomenon, historically speaking, and watching Beth die so selflessly seems to release a rush of guilt in many of us for being the aggressive women we have conscientiously trained ourselves to be. Males cannot be counted in the equation since so few make it to Beth's death in a conscious state.

But even during the low point of my early twenties, it was only in the play I wanted to be Beth. My choice of who to be in real life was never Beth, though I have met other women, smart women with successful careers, who gladly choose Beth, willing to suffer the rather dire consequences of such a choice in exchange for—what? The no-one-expects-you-to-have-a-thought-in-your-head-ness that looks so relaxing? The total absence of one single unsaintly thought? The attention or approval they never got as a child? Of course nobody ever got enough approval as a child, but evidently I wasn't willing to die for that in my preteen youth, because at eleven I had chosen distinctly and vociferously to be Amy: the pretty, get-me-out-of-this-popcorn-stand blonde—who, in defiance of Marmee's maxims, dares to spend a penny on herself for perfume. Dreary, virtuous fates await her sisters, but the selfish Amy gets everything. She gets a rich aunt to take her instead of Jo to Europe; she gets to marry Laurie, the handsome rich boy next door; she gets to live in a nice house without worrying about making ends meet. Like Amy, I had been breathless with greed ever since I could remember. Like Amy, I had been told that that was wrong. I wanted to be Amy because Amy had sprung free.

That was before I reread *Little Women* as a mother of three and was shaken with self-revelatory horror at my choice. Amy—who spitefully burns Jo's manuscript (after which *Jo* gets the lecture from Marmee on controlling her anger). Amy—who is vain, pretentious, and mercenary; who has no qualms about marrying a man for his money; who is stupidly snobbish and mean. Amy, who is guiltless about it all. Even Louisa with her considerable powers cannot redeem Amy with hasty remarks shoved in near the end of the book about how Amy was softened by her love for rich Laurie—who *wouldn't* be softened by all that cash?— as well as by the death of her sister Beth—for whom Amy does not cut short her European vacation by one day. This time through, I thought: *Why not Jo?!* Who is so driven and misunderstood and guilty, guilty, guilty, but who has a talent that takes her over (no writer's block for Jo!). And yet— she marries Professor Bhaer! As old as her father, and even less fun—musty and poor, with a German accent, and spouting more moralisms than Marmee on a bad day. And back to the shallow waters of Amy I slunk.

LOUISA WROTE the first half of what she called "my stupid Little Women" mechanically, too quickly, and for the money. She and the publisher had agreed that it was a little "dull."

And they were right. Part One of *Little Women* is a little dull. I concluded this one evening when the phone rang for me and Charlie was left to read the goody-goody first chapter to seven-year-old Emily, lifting a shell-shocked face to me when I returned as he closed the book forever, breathing, "I had *no* idea." A few years earlier, I had tried bribing ten-year-old Teddy to read the book with a $10 bill. "It's a great book," I told Teddy, just as I had ventured with sinking heart to tell eleven-year-old Hunter, clad in a self-decorated T-shirt with a girl's face X'ed out, in case you are foreign and cannot read the "I hate grils" (*sic*) written in indelible marker above. But Teddy was unable to contain his horror as he followed me around the house turning the pages. "Slang, slang, they call *this* slang?" he called out derisively, and was out the door with "A *merry* Christmas?!!! *And they're not getting any presents?!*"—before I could cry out, "Wait, wait, Beth is going to die!"

For when Beth dies, in Part Two, *Little Women* rises above its saccharine moralities to become something great. Rereading the book as an adult, the year we'd moved to Nashawtuc Hill, I was shocked by its banality—until I found myself on page 59 unable to suppress my sniffling. Just knowing Beth's end lay ahead, I burst into tears and was unable to read on without biting a wet facecloth. I was at the part where Beth (who isn't sick yet, but anyone in the know is simply waiting for a telltale cough from page 1) gets the piano from Laurie's grandfather, and, though shy to the point of psychosis, runs next door to hug the old man, who had once had a beloved granddaughter, we learn, who died young, etc., etc. Later, when Beth does sicken, I had to lock myself in the bathroom with my makeup streaming down my face, lest my children glimpse their mother's naked face. I did not care when the father was off possibly dying in the Civil War (the true fact that the author's father lolled about at home was like steel in my heart), but in the last chapter when it is mentioned that Amy's daughter has the same too-good-for-this-world fragility as her aunt Beth, I started up again, streaming right through Marmee holding out her arms for her girls.

Even when I knew so much of it was untrue:

In the novel, Beth dies after her sisters blow off a visit to the poor neighbors, whose baby sickens of scarlet fever as a result, then dies after infecting Beth. But in real life, it was Marmee, whose caring of Boston's poor in the Alcotts' city home had contaminated Beth; Marmee, whose slack nursing the doctor blamed when it was clear that Beth would never get well. Poor Marmee, who had been so disapproving of Lidian Emerson's mothering skills when her own little boy had died of the same disease, now found herself similarly accused.

In real life, Beth had not died in romantic Orchard House, but in a rented room in Concord, where she'd been hauled on the heels of Bronson's latest real estate project: the decrepit Orchard House, purchased after the Alcotts had finally managed to unload Hillside (on Nathaniel Hawthorne). Beth had died before they'd moved in, her coffin carried to Sleepy Hollow by Thoreau and Emerson.

In real life, next door was not the handsome, rich Laurie, but the miserable Hawthorne. Hawthorne, who'd been abroad when he'd bought Hillside, had never imagined the Alcotts would soon be moving next door (where Orchard House rather inconveniently was). In the years he lived there, Hawthorne would only visit the Alcotts twice, unable to bear the "booming voice" of Mrs. Alcott.

And in real life the sweet dying Beth was not quite so sweet, but bald and cranky, suffering from ether withdrawal and calling Anna horrid and not letting Marmee near.

But I don't care. The death of Beth in *Little Women* is the one true scene of the book.

Louisa would destroy whole years of her journals for being too personal. But it is her personal entry the day Beth died—much of which she allowed to appear in *Little Women*—that moves me most:

March 14. My dear Beth died at three this morning. . . . Last week she put her work away, saying the needle was "too heavy," and having given us her few possessions, made ready for the parting in her own simple, quiet way. For two days she suffered much, begging for ether. . . . Saturday she slept . . . quietly breathing her life away till three; then, with one last look of the beautiful eyes, she was gone. . . . For the last time we dressed her in her usual cap and gown, and laid her on her bed—at rest at last. . . . [A]t twenty-three she looked like a woman of forty . . . all her pretty hair gone.

Bronson's real estate–ish journal entry the night Beth was dying is a bit less moving: "Bricklayer builds the west parlour fireplace, fashioning it after my design, the bricks projecting from the jambs and forming an arch. Garfield trails mason."

WITHOUT BETH'S DEATH, there would be no long lines of Japanese tourists at Orchard House. And no out-of-town retirees, the men with blank, mystified faces, wondering why they are here and when they get to eat again, as they are ushered past the harsh photographs into the dark, dingy, hovelish "modern" kitchen designed by Bronson ("the first househusband!" one tour guide said recently). Without Beth dead, the children of Concord wouldn't have to stand year after year in that supposedly shabby (but actually rather English Country) dining room where brave little Beth's piano sits (although, in reality, brave little Beth never sat there herself, being six feet under). Without Beth's early death, my children would not have been accosted in elementary school by middle-aged adults who travel about this town dressed as the Alcotts, asking the $80-Nike-shod children, "Oh my, did no one come in barefoot today?" So that Hunter in the fourth grade had cried, "Bring back the discovery of America again, anything but this!" But not, however, Emily when she is nine. "Why was Mr. Pollet laughing when the Alcotts came to class today?" she asks. No, not Emily. Even at age five, when I dragged her to see the new film version, with Susan Sarandon as Marmee ("If she takes her shirt off, I'll go," Charlie had said, "otherwise forget it"), and the entire story flew over her head, she whispered to me at the end, "Mommy, I liked it when the girl died."

Without Beth's death, *Little Women* would not have moved millions and made millions and kept Concord on the map. Without Beth's death, the fantasy of *Little Women* would not have rung real. Without Beth's death, I would not have returned so gloriously and pathetically to my hometown, hoping to recapture a coziness that nobody ever had.

CHAPTER SEVENTEEN

MY LITTLE
WOMEN (1990s)

ONE EMOTION MODERN CHILDREN are spared is how it feels to pick up a phone and be hit with the wobbling surprise that it's your mother on the other end. I resisted installing Caller ID for years, shocked by its inherent cruelty after it was installed on Hunter and Teddy's landline. "Isobel called twenty-two times," Teddy reported casually

*Our house on Nashawtuc Hill, after we had fixed it
up with a kitchen so cozy, I think of it daily.*

to Hunter about Hunter's long-term girlfriend, recently "dumped."

And so when I picked up the phone one morning to hear my mother's voice, I felt the usual surge of trepidation, which the excitement in my mother's voice turned to a queasy hope. I should have known better. In all the years of my mother calling to say, "I have some good news," too often it had not been good news about me but good news about a sibling, or some other rival for my mother's approval. "I have something special for you. Can I bring it over today at two when you've finished work?" my mother asked. I had once told my parents I worked from ten to two, and forever after my mother would call me at the stroke of two, always remembering to ask, "How's your little project coming along?" as if I had been cutting things out for a scrapbook. My mother dropping by for a visit meant that I had to brush the dog hairs from the living room sofa and poison the kitchen countertops with Fantastik until my hands were as dry and chapped and intermittently bleeding as Scarlett O'Hara's in Rhett Butler's prison cell. Because the truth is, Lidian Emerson and our Puritan forebears were right: there *is* an un-Godly shame in a messy house, as if one's inner ugliness were on display.

Who are those women who declare joyfully, "I'm *so* excited, my mother is coming to lunch tomorrow!"? Not New

England women—at least not many. Mother-daughter love is complicated at best, and in Protestant New England it pulses with the anxiety of never measuring up. When I think of those sunny, hopeful afternoon visits from my beautiful mother to my beautiful house; when I think of how much it meant for my mother not just to have her daughter living in town with her, but to be able to tell people she did; when I think of how soon I too will be gathering up the crumbs of my grown children's time and affection to store for barren days; when I remember the glow of joy on my mother's face as she came up my walk—I am filled with profound regret and shame. My mother didn't ask for much and I was unable to give her even that.

I had come back to Concord to feel the warmth of my parents' approval running over me like hot fudge on vanilla ice cream. Under my parents' guidelines, if not my own, I had overachieved. And yet, even living on Nashawtuc Hill, basking in my parents' pride, I sometimes dreaded my mother's appearance in my day-to-day life. Idling at the computer on a weekday morning, I would gaze out the window to see a brand-new, hideously aquamarine Ford Taurus (which *Newsweek*, on the heels of my parents' purchase, had pronounced the least likely car to be stolen in a parking lot) appearing in my driveway, every single time thinking, *Who in the world do I know who would drive that fakely jazzy car,* only to see—my parents! Getting out and moving phalanx-like toward my door, stopping by for "just a minute," rendering the rest of my working day useless. My impossibly good-looking, bright-faced, kindhearted, anxious-to-please parents, shooting up in a flash from the sofa after a ten-minute visit, careful not to impose, grateful to salvage a scrap of news about our "interesting" lives. If only my mother had known how the merest implied criticism of something as trivial as my hair could sink my spirits for a week. If only my well-meaning, beloved mother had known—if only I had told her—that behind all the migraines of my return to Concord was the fear of her rejection.

But still I could not help wondering about my mother's great surprise. *Could it be . . . a check? Uncharacteristic for sure, but since Charlie and I were going down the tubes, surely possible. Or perhaps it was a piece of furniture or silver?* For the signs of wealth will ever be more comforting to me than the wealth itself. But when my mother arrived on my porch with her special surprise, it was not a suitcase of money but two prettily wrapped boxes with bows. My parents had always been no-nonsense about gifts and their accoutrements. There had never been any Santa stickers or little bells or swirling bows, the card itself was their own invention of folded wrapping paper. We were not a present-y family—our discomfort tracing back to the Puritans who made a point—though what point I do not know—of treating Christmas like an ordinary day. "What do you want for your birthday, Mommy?" was always answered with "Something you make yourself," though among the six of us spun not one electron of craftsmanship. And so the fudge that didn't harden was curled up in foil and presented in a coffee can, or the star-shaped ashtray was sprayed with gold glitter and bestowed upon the nonsmoking parents. As adults, the concept of giving someone a present still fills my brothers and me with turmoil and dread. Even I, the show-off, cannot order a gift from a wedding registry without what my great-grandparents used to call "a sick headache." The last time my married brothers and I exchanged gifts was thirty years ago per a no-gift agreement no sister-in-law has been able to undo. When my parents were informed that a recently remarried son wished them to consider his new teenage stepdaughters as grandchildren, my parents, though they dearly loved the girls, had not been able to contain their chagrin, crying out piteously from time to time, "Now we have *nine* grandchildren to buy presents for!"

But that afternoon on the living room couch sat two presents out of the blue, practically illegal, and next to them, perched expectantly, my mother, beaming with pride. With an embarrassed smile I opened them to find—was this possible from my stylish mother to her black-jeaned daughter?—Laura Ashley mother-daughter dresses for Emily and me, festooned with ribbons and lace and flowers bigger than those on the late Queen Mum's hat. "You always said you wanted a mother-daughter outfit when you were little," my mother gushed. *Yes*, I wanted to cry out, *I had wanted it when I was little*—"and," she continued, "I never let you have one!"—*and you were right!* I longed to add. But I seldom said a true thing to my mother. So instead, with a heavy heart I could not disguise, I donned the baby-doll shirtwaist dress with the giant white collar and ribbon sash, making neither my mother nor me happy, but only (at least for an exclusive one-time-only engagement of one half hour in her room) Emily.

I weep to think of these last years with my parents, begun on such a high for us all. Age had mellowed my mother, and, perhaps more important, her friends' growing (if qualified) acceptance of her suddenly respectable Concord daughter had allowed her to lower her guard with me. In the end, my mother's disapproval of her children had sprung from her own low self-esteem and desire for acceptance. At last, the "shouldn'ts" had begun to dissipate; she could turn to me without the constraints that had held me close but kept me distant. Finally she could unleash the demonstrations of affection that she had thought spoiling to lavish on me when I was a child. But try as I might, I could not accept them.

But Emily could, and so Emily became the conduit.

My mother had always considered herself "a baby person." Her only paying job had been in the 1960s, working, for $7 a week, in the Sunday school nursery at Trinity Church. She often spoke of her girlhood dream of having eleven children, and though the four she had had nearly killed her, her ardor for grandchildren had not been dampened. But when at last the grandson babies had come, my mother had been too cautious: desperate for a hug but standing back because she "didn't want to force it." Emily was her last chance, and my mother had screwed up her courage and boldly reached for her in infancy. She'd rocked her and wrapped her tenderly in her hooded towel after her bath and warmed her own sunset-pink, crease-softened cheek next to the rosy warmth of Emily's. The boys had played raucously outside, but inside, the old grandfather clock had ticked its old-fashioned comfort while Emily and my mother had played before the fire, Emily, in a long be-ribboned dress, climbing in and out of my mother's lap to bring her favored stuffed animals, to gently pat my mother's hair with her silver-plated baby's brush, as picturesque as a little woman by a hearthside Marmee. Emily and my mother were to be as close as my mother and her own mother had never been, was the unspoken theory, and as close as my mother and I had never been. With Emily, my mother would even be—generous. She would rise above three hundred years of proud retention, defy the sanctity of a penny saved, break through everything that had repressed her from the cradle, and bring Emily $4 gifts every now and then, *for no reason at all*. Breathless in her audacity, my mother would descend upon us with a wild eye, smiling as if her face would break, to bestow upon Emily the little pink plastic mirror or fake fairy-sprinkled lipstick. But I could see the hammer crashing down on the anvil that was her brain, pounding in the guilt of this blasphemous act. For what of the other grandchildren who didn't get $4 gifts *for-absolutely-no-reason?*

Through Emily we played out our *Little Women* fantasy of cozy affection. But like the nonfiction Marmee, my mother was too burdened by the past and present to play it out as often as she wished. When I pulled Emily out of the too-cooperative nursery school at age three, my mother begged to take her three mornings a week, and then, well, two mornings, or at least Fridays, but barely a week passed without a calamity intervening. One morning I was called to be told, "You'll *never* guess what happened," both parents on the phone breathing in solemn tones as if they'd lost a child instead of their address book. Or my mother couldn't take Emily because her back was out or she had to decorate thirty lunch bags for the Cripple School ladies committee or finish up the illegible personalized Christmas cards that had plagued my parents' lives for half a century. Or my mother couldn't do anything for a month because, after years and years of silversmithing classes, she had been "commissioned" (though of course, she would *never* accept money for it) to make a silver "J" for a friend's daughter's birthday. "That J!'" my father would cry out in despair whenever I called.

And then, periodically my mother fell into deep depressions—depressions I had either never known of or she had been able to suppress in the early days when she had been running the home show of suppers and kids; depressions which in our teens she had risen above in the crises of her own children's mental breakdowns. But when the domestic game should have been over—won or lost or tied, who cared, just over!; when my mother had moved to assisted living, relieving her of the essential bane of figuring out meals and weeding the garden; when even the eternal money problems were past; when her only obligation was to live a nice life; when my mother, like Lidian Emerson, should have at last found joy—the depressions came on fast and furious. A week of polite excuses would be made until my father would call distraught and I would be summoned over to see my mother, my poor, striving-to-be-good mother, dissolved in hopeless tears, in her perfectly appointed, all-white, mirror-walled apartment.

AND WHY couldn't I have enfolded my weeping mother in my arms? Why couldn't I have taken my mother into my heart instead of steeling it against her? Why couldn't I have once been honest, instead of polite and considerate, but never kind? Why couldn't I have seen that the conflicts she struggled against were my conflicts too, that my mother needed my love as much as I needed hers? Because of that great New Englander spoiler: money.

After my mother inherited money and had no more excuses, her continued frugality felt like a knife to the heart. I realize now that my mother's frugality was no different than the proud, silly, endearing thrift of her friends. No different, for that matter, than my father's frugality. But it was always my mother I blamed. I felt that if I asked, my father would give me everything.

I was embarrassed when she loaned me $2,000 when we were broke instead of giving it to me: when she asked me for payment on the first day of the first indebted month, I borrowed from the bank to pay her back. I couldn't forgive her when she made remarks about a small loan to a son and how loaning more would simply be throwing good money after bad. I was mortified when she charged us 6.4 percent interest. I wondered—unfairly—if I were starving in the streets whether my mother would give me money or, Marmee-like, decide to let me learn my lesson at the soup kitchen for my own good. "But you've lived on money you didn't earn your whole life!" I wanted to cry out. And if I'd been able to, honest arguments would have saved my mother and me from a lot of needless pain. But I was too afraid to try.

I was too anxious to see that the sudden windfall had filled my mother with so much confused mortification that she had had no choice but to hang on ever more fiercely to the penny-wisdom that had been calming New Englanders for centuries. It was as if frugality, the counting and recounting of money, was an obsessive disorder for Protestant guilt. The inherited money made her more worried and more careful, so that even on the sacred ground of my mother's love for Emily, now sneaked in the accounting, the God-directed need to show thrift, to be even-steven. One December day, long after my parents had inherited a million dollars, I came home to find a message from my mother on the machine explaining that while they had bought Emily an audiotape recorder for her Christmas present, they hadn't been able to afford the $6 *Lion King* tape to put in it. At first I was confused, knowing that the tape recorder had cost $40 and that my parents spent exactly $50 per grandchild at Christmas. Then I remembered the gingerbread house that had arrived the day before and realized it had been "charged" to Emily's account.

CHAPTER EIGHTEEN

MY UTOPIA

NOT LONG AGO, as I walked with my friend Kay around Nashawtuc Hill, I felt a Marmee-like indignation rising in my soul, as blondes in their thirties sprinted by with bare midriffs and jogging strollers, hastening home for morning meetings with landscape architects. "Used to be, a block party meant you walked your gin and tonic next door," Kay sighed. That year, the block party on Nashawtuc Hill

---

The new rich were taking over Nashawtuc Hill, tearing houses to the ground and pumping up others to twice, sometimes three times, their size.

had organizing committees and mailed invitations, an ice-cream truck, and a magician. Surely, if not slowly, the new rich were taking over Nashawtuc Hill, pumping up the houses to twice, sometimes thrice their size. And unlike the development-mansion mothers of Hunter's and Teddy's youth, these mothers were not temporary dwellers with upwardly mobile husbands waiting for reassignment. They were here to stay: buying houses for millions of dollars and tearing them to ground, spending so much money to rebuild them that their investment could never be recouped in a hundred years.

The hill was as deafening on a weekday morning as Midtown Manhattan. Monstrous machinery moved monstrous chunks of land; trucks ground and clanked, beeping to and fro; drills mimed the rat-tat-tat of hell; whole houses and lawns and fifty-year-old trees were lifted into the air. But the loudest whir was in my brain, trying to do the math on the elegant Victorian of Hunter's first girlfriend, that had been under full-scale reconstruction, lo, the past four years—no end in sight. Sold for $2.9 million, it had been knocked down to the studs, the fine mahogany library paneling tossed willy-nilly with giant splats into the overflowing dumpster. Next to this bomb-site sat an expensive, pseudo-historic sign saying, PLEASE PARDON OUR RESTORATION.

But the truth was, those owners didn't need my pardon, because I am sure that I, also, would have spent a huge amount of money on that house, if the money had been made available to me. Gladly would I have braved the no-nonsense Concordians huffing disapproval as they walked their dogs around the construction projects on Nashawtuc Hill; gladly would I have weathered my own self-condemnation—for such a house!

And then my moral indignation against the rich was suspect for another reason: we had not lasted long on Nashawtuc Hill. After four short years, we sold the house because, even after Charlie's work had picked up, we couldn't meet the mortgage.

IN THE FOUR YEARS we lived on Nashawtuc Hill, I lost the confidence of my sons; bought groceries on credit for a year; reread *Little Women*; became clinically depressed because we couldn't afford the $10,000 initiation fee to join a country club we never used; told my parents how I really felt about them in a nonfiction book; created a kitchen so cozy I think of it daily; sold our house because we had to, and lied about the reason why.

And still I wish I could relive it all again. Back then, at least the feelings ran deep and the audience was wide. At least then, if there was absence of hope, there was hope of its return. At least if my sons were gone in spirit they were still at the breakfast table.

Come back, Hunter and Teddy, boisterous beacons of success in their bowl-cut haircuts, on the cusp of leaving me forever—for girls, skateboards, and stolen bottles of Tanqueray. Come back, Teddy at eleven, surprised by his mother one weekday morning pouring Saturday-only "dessert cereal" into his bowl, tapping his head in a mimed *geez* at his forgetfulness, then carefully pouring the cereal back into its box. Come back, Hunter at twelve, running home after school convulsed with hatred for a terrible girl he called "Thing" at the new bus stop, and me carefully agreeing with him, only to have a sultry beauty show up a few days later, Teddy remarking, "Don't look now, but Thing's playing basketball with Hunter."

Come back, even the middle school years—when Charlie's and my sense of humor was as missing in action as our understanding; when Hunter and Teddy spoke to us only administratively, with the occasional "I don't think I want to be smart" tossed in; when both boys quit reading (for my benefit) and sports (for Charlie's benefit); when the other mothers, once so chatty and monitoring of their fresh-cheeked children, dropped their surly skateboarding progeny off for weekends like ticking time bombs, without getting out of the car.

And—come back, Emily, during those four golden years. Emily, dressed in purple and pink, carrying a My Little Pony boom box blaring Carly Simon's sexual come-ons: *"Do the walls come down when you think of me."* Come back, Emily, before she too became a teenager and had to get into college and suddenly felt not quite so brilliant as her parents had always told her she was. Come back, five-year-old Emily, clasping my hand tightly, a tear trickling down her cheek as she tells me that if I die, she wants to die with me! And then the next day, Emily skipping up the stairs saying joyously to a friend, "Let's pretend our mothers are dead and Miss Patricia is our mother!" Come back, Emily, in the third grade's four-hour talent show, where no child is left behind and why not, when mouthing the same sexually explicit Britney Spears song with sulky stamps and unsynchronized JonBenét wriggles is greeted with the thunderous applause of a thousand parents. Come back, Emily, who has never wanted to leave me, but who must leave me now.

Come back, the disapprovers! Mrs. Glowers and all my mother's Concord friends, walking toward me in the woods or on the streets with furrowed brows, because I have written a nonfiction book about my family. Come back, all the guilt-sinking days of that book that I so genius-like (though the opposite of a genius) felt inspired to write, delving into the history of my relatives—all so eager to talk and to be transcribed but then queasy to see their stories published. Come back, the book in galleys, which line by line I went over with my parents for a month, the one headache-free month of my life—because for once I was being truthful with my mother—but the worst. Come back, the next fall and winter and spring, when my mother, so private about her feelings but so forthcoming in her interviews, cannot not sit quietly in church without being accosted by a stranger saying, "I read your daughter's book!" Come back, that terrible day at the Concord Book-shop when I read my analysis of my parents to my parents, and watched their bright smiles tighten. Come back, my parents.

Come back, even, our last year on the hill: when the house reeked of Old Spice and unwashed gym clothes. When rap music pounded through walls, or streamed through earbuds at the dinner table. When laundry was piled up undone in the boys' rooms, or done one piece at a time. When trails of smoke-y adolescents sneaked in and out like thieves, even in the bright of day. When, adhering to the mothering tenet I held sacrosanct—that the kids always be allowed to tell me what they thought about me—I finally coaxed out of a fourteen-year-old son a mumbled, "You (expletive) bricks," and had answered brightly, "Well, okay, that's a start!"

I would relive it all again. After all the years of positive reinforcing (even when suddenly there had been nothing positive to reinforce), after all the years of trying to avoid the guilt-tripping traps of my parents' parenting, I would rush back through time to be told by Hunter and Teddy, "You're so judgmental!" Gladly would I rewatch my boys become unrecognizable and turn from me, rewatch Charlie lose his confidence and my parents the fullness of my love. I would turn back the clock to that terrible time, when I was happy even when I was unhappy, because we still lived on Nashawtuc Hill.

For just as John Winthrop's Puritans lived righteously in their "city on the hill" for all the world to emulate, so the Nashawtuc Hill old-guard residents had quietly lived their greedless, unimpeachable lives with nothing to hide. And for me, living among these upright Concordians—who had been protected by God for so long that they seemed spared the vicissitudes of ordinary life; who had nothing to prove and nothing to earn; whose success was so rooted in the past as to be deemed irrelevant; who might suffer, but never despair; who, blessed enough to live in this heaven on earth, surely will graduate after their toils to the real thing—it was hard not to believe that I too would always be safe.

CHAPTER NINETEEN

HOMESICK I

"MOTHER'S Day is just an invention of the florists," I had been told over and over growing up. One Mother's Day, after our Irish babysitter had sent her mother a check for $1,000, I had caved, daring to buy my mother a $20 photograph album, driving it over to my parents' to show them how I saved on postage. In return had come the long letter from my mother. "I love you, darling, but I am very worried

---

*Thoreau's 15-by-10-foot cabin. The secret to entertaining—
Thoreau rather brilliantly advised—is never to
mention "dinner."*

about the way you are with money and think you should see a psychiatrist about it . . ."

A decade later, I took my parents and Emily and Charlie to a $400 Mother's Day brunch at the Ritz that Charlie, the most generous husband alive, will never his long life forget: sometimes a certain expression sets upon his face and I know he is remembering. But for my mother—no flowers or candy please, but a $400 brunch tab she had accepted as graciously as if she were a head of state who never carried her own purse. It turned out that though the tiniest outlay of money for presents was frowned upon, it was perfectly okay to spend a wad taking one's parents to a restaurant. Apparently, a lavish meal out was one of the loopholes of being a WASP, like drinking alcohol.

Whether that brunch sends me to heaven or hell, I can only say it was a necessity at the time, to make up to my parents for what I had written about them. "The part that hurts the most," my mother said as I took my parents laboriously through the manuscript, "is that you think love is money." And my sweet father had written me a letter that if I published the book, they would have to leave Concord.

FAILING IN YOUR HOMETOWN is hard for anyone; in New England, it's not just hard, it's defining. For Henry Thoreau, who lived and died in his mother's house, it was debilitating.

From the only child she sent to Harvard, Cynthia Thoreau had expected more return than what she seemed to get: a guy who taught a little, surveyed a little, and picnicked a lot. The outdoors was all very well, but somehow a son who thought collecting huckleberries on a summer afternoon the absolute *height* of life—well, it was impossible that she would understand. Cynthia might have enjoyed shocking the town with her critical remarks, but she craved the prestige and material success the town recognized.

Fortunately, Thoreau had written a few drafts of his second book, *Walden*, before his first book flopped, or *Walden* might never have been written. What writer has the strength to plunge forward excitedly into a second book when the first book, about which your fame was to be proclaimed from land to land, falls with a quiet thud into oblivion. His first book, *A Week on the Concord and Merrimack Rivers*, was published at Thoreau's expense (with help from Emerson) in 1849. The book had been declined by every publisher it had been submitted to—jammed as it was with everything Thoreau could dream up, including a hundred unattributed quotes; some highfalutin nonsense on friendship and love from a man who understood little about either ("True love does not quarrel for slight reasons"—fact-check this with any married person); and some of the most beautiful writing linking nature and history I have ever read.

A Week was supposed to exonerate Thoreau from charges of being a ne'er-do-well. It was supposed to give him the fame and status that would replace money as a sign of election in the eyes of his mother, the town, and the Puritan God he had tried to flee. Instead, it garnered mixed reviews and dismal sales. After hauling back the unsold copies, Thoreau wrote, "I now have a library of over nine hundred books, over seven hundred of them I have written myself." He also maintained, in that way of his, that the book's failure was a good thing: "I believe that this result is more inspiring and better for me than if a thousand had bought my wares. It affects my privacy less and leaves me freer." And yet, it is hard not to feel Thoreau's humiliation. One townsman said, "This strange man, rumor said, had written a book, no copy of which has ever been sold."

Today, of course, Thoreau has a greater presence in Concord than any other Concord author, eclipsing even the busloads of bemused international tourists bound inexplicably for the home of Louisa May Alcott. Even the most recent transplant sporting a Lexus SUV with video backup is comfortable dropping the name of the great simplifier. And why not, for it has never been necessary to read

Thoreau to quote him. Thoreau's name adorns shops (THO-
REALLY ANTIQUES), societies, awards, schools, church circu-
lars, college essays, and titles of books in which Thoreau
does not appear.

And yet, despite the current fashionableness of Thoreau, I have realized since I returned to town that most
Concordians don't really like him. Not that we don't agree
that his ever-widening fame is a nice reflection upon the
town and so forth. Not that there isn't a certain refined
group who can always be called upon to quaff cheap white
wine and taste-free cheese rectangles on his fund-raising
behalf. Not that he wasn't a fine writer (just don't make us
read him). Still, we just can't help but be irritably surprised
at his popularity in the world beyond. It is like watching
the growing fame of a once-deadbeat sibling. In this town,
we know him too well and not well enough.

And yet Concord's latent antipathy for Thoreau does
not quite explain the unbecoming fact that Thoreau had
been pissing me off since the day I got off the school bus at
Walden Pond for those excruciating swimming lessons.
Once I had been proud of my aversion, but my increasing
knowledge—in that tricky way knowledge has of mucking
up one's cherished prejudices—has only made me wonder
why my feelings had always been so violent. Whether it's
because Thoreau exemplifies the judgmental quality I can't

stand (but am the personification of); or because I'm a girl (now mother) who (still) likes a pretty bedroom; or because in the end unless I own it, I don't care all that much about nature; or because Thoreau was foisted upon me as a child—I cannot yet tell you.

But I can tell you that (finally) reading Thoreau's books is not what has changed my mind. It's when I read *about* Thoreau that I love him—less for his independence than for his dependence, less for his virtues than his weaknesses. How can I not love and pity Thoreau? He was as neurotically attached to his mother and childhood and hometown as I am. Even the cabin at Walden was only a mile and a half from his mother's house, where almost every day he stopped in for a meal (if not at Emerson's or the Alcotts'). When Thoreau states in *Walden* that it is the coward who travels thousands of miles to go to war and the brave one who stays home to look within—one can't help but ask, *How on earth would Thoreau have known?* It may have been hard, even humiliating, for Thoreau to live at home his adult life, but it wasn't brave. And whether it was his mother Thoreau couldn't leave, or Concord, can never be known, since he predeceased his mother. Perhaps his mother's death would have released him from the intoxication of this small, enchanting town and set him free.

It's hard to believe you are great when your father makes

pencils and not as cleverly as you do, and your dissatisfied mother is the village gossip, and Emerson, your mentor, is disappointed, and your townsmen think you're lazy. Even *Walden* wasn't a vindication at the time; it got good reviews, but only two thousand copies were printed (at Thoreau's expense). In the eight years Thoreau had left to live, it's no wonder he was unable to pull a third book together. It wasn't until 1861, when *Walden* was suddenly slated for a second printing, that Thoreau was again possessed by the feverish inspiration that can only come from self-belief. Unfortunately, he was dying—at age forty-four.

MY NONFICTION BOOK about the family poet whose poetry I didn't understand was a commercial flop as well, but unlike Thoreau's books, it was a success in Concord— meaning *The New York Times* and my parents' friends liked it. Instead of leaving town, my father now found himself wandering into the bookstore waiting to be recognized. Even the Glowers, who had frowned so thunderously when they'd heard the book's subtitle contained the words "money" and "madness" and "family," changed their tune after reading a glowing article in *The Boston Globe.* "Why don't you write about *our* family?" they blurted out as they passed me on Nashawtuc Road.

For a few short months, I even sauntered around town, modestly smiling at everyone. My heart rose, instead of froze, in the supermarket to spot Mrs. Darling down aisle 4. Mrs. Darling!—the esteemed Concord matriarch, so tough to please, her children would not be able to suppress the breath of relief from their emotional eulogies several years later. Once, I would have ducked down another aisle at the sight of Mrs. Darling sternly comparing prices, but Mrs. Darling had been at the bookstore for my reading that Saturday. So when I heard her clarion voice addressing me, not by my childhood nickname, but at last, at last(!), by my writing name—"Sarah Payne Stuart!"—I had whirled around aglow, only to hear her exclaim, "You have my cart."

Then Charlie had told me we had to sell the house on Nashawtuc Hill. "We don't approve of you selling the house," my parents said, even after Charlie wrote them it was a financial necessity. "What can we tell our friends?" In the end, despite their stated belief that money was not important, my parents had been proud of me for seeming to have it, by living on Nashawtuc Hill. And when we had to move, they were ashamed. And so was I.

CHAPTER TWENTY

HOMESICK II

I CAME BACK TO MY HOMETOWN to give my children the childhood I thought I'd had. For the reality was, my childhood, on the closest examination, wasn't quite as stunningly perfect as I kept painting for my children. Despite proclaiming to the uninterested group in the backseat, "That's where Ranger, the Moultons' dog, got run over," the truth was that I'd been homesick from birth, shuttled

---

The river overflow below Nashawtuc Hill—here, one cold winter, Thoreau, Hawthorne, and Emerson skated together, Thoreau executing "Bacchic leaps on the ice. . . ."

between relatives; that when my mother had returned from the hospital, my brothers had fought one another for her love, while I'd fought merely for her presence; that nursery school had been a blur because I needed glasses; that the first-grade teacher had thought me stupid because I had been too shy to mention I couldn't see the blackboard. That I'd been anemic and withdrawn till the fourth grade. That every day when I'd come home from school I'd feared my brothers would kill one another, knives displayed from under their pillows for my personal viewing. That family car trips had sometimes resulted with a brother getting out on a highway median to run away. That my mother had always battled depression, something I had never dreamed of until I moved back to Concord, that she would always love me with all the love a mother can have, but despite all the psychiatry in the world, this I would never believe. That we had been a family struggling—for money, normalcy, and happiness. And that it had been the year I was twelve, when Johnny had been a senior in high school and pride of the town, that the family had briefly triumphed.

Apparently, I moved back to Concord because I had a good year in the sixth grade. This at least is left: the fact that in the sixth grade, Sam Wells (now dead of a brain tumor) and Donnie Delmara, best friends of each other, were boyfriends of mine, courting me simultaneously, flanking me as we biked to school, presenting me with rival animal pins to wear on my lapel; the fact that my brother was not yet in the mental hospital; the fact that my hair still worked. I shall gloss over the D in handwriting ("The first D in the family," my father intoned gloomily), which, to be honest, was far more traumatic than the death that year of my grandmother, which, with its little surge of money, slides over to the plus column.

In the sixth grade, my school was in the center of town—no wonder we were happy. No thief, no adulterer, no homeless person could spring from the security of this Protestant Disneyland, where people whistled on the way to the bank. In the sixth grade, the bell would sound and we would flow, sparkling with high spirits, out the double doors and into the afternoon sunlight, and down the hard, pounded-dirt sidewalks to the center of town. We would pass the brick, pillared library—where high school students studied and flirted between busts of Transcendentalists; where my father's pamphlets "Businessman's Banjo" and "Instant Uke" had graced the Concord authors shelf along with Emerson and Thoreau; where my unlocked bike could rust in the outside rack for days with impunity. On this land had stood one of Thoreau's mother Cynthia's boardinghouses, the pencil factory in the back, grinding so much graphite it coated the piano and the family's tubercular lungs. We would buy a cookie from Sally Ann's on our way to Woolworth's (replaced in the 1980s by Irresistibles), where my goldfish, Jo and Laurie, had been bought and bagged and christened, only to expire on the way home. At Woolworth's, a dollar bought you a zippered pencil case with a girl in pedal pushers and a ponytail lounging on the front. At Woolworth's, the lunch counter was filled with old people eating scoops of tuna fish, and working people in custodial uniforms smoking over empty coffee saucers, and at 3:10 p.m., Monday through Friday, with my friends and me, eating French fries with ketchup in a paper cone.

We had our own building that year, we sixth graders. There were no pubescent seventh graders and eighth graders to mar those fleeting days when our bodies were straight and our skins pure. The Peter Bulkeley School—named for the Puritan reverend—was across from the fields and tennis courts of Emerson Playground. Once it had been a proud new high school. Then—replaced by the proud newer Emerson High School—it had been demoted to junior high; and finally superannuated into a spill-over school building for the sixth grade. The Peter Bulkeley building was deemed unmodern, hopelessly antiquated with its cavernous center hallway and sweeping staircase and large, glorious double-hung windows—an eyesore in the 1960s when cheap modernity reigned supreme. But not to us. We filled its caverns with the unfettered joy of sixth-grade children with warm houses and housewife mothers in them awaiting our return.

Even now I am envisioning myself back on Emerson Playground at recess as the crowd swarms into cliques. The September sky, the exciting hum of two hundred twelve-year-olds after the dull buzz of summer, happily sweating in our new fall clothes. The smart girls ("the brains") and the popular girls and the "cheapies" still together, still blissfully unaware of who they are, before the great divide of seventh grade, when classes were tracked and futures preordained. In those days, where kids were placed seemed to reflect the division of the east side of town, with its older, grander houses, from the west, with its farms and old mill town. If you lived in the east, your address was "Concord"; in the west, "West Concord." The school tracking system had probably evolved from the unspoken New England premise that the rich (people living near Concord Center) were smarter than the unrich (millworkers and farmers living in the west).

But this snobbish theory had been dealt an irreparable blow with the advent of the genius Leviten children. The Levitens, along with other families of MIT and Harvard professors, had arrived in town in the 1960s, buying houses in the appealingly rustic development which had recently been built in a woodsy part of West Concord along the river, to which Thoreau had given the Indian-ish—but actually derived from Conant who owned the land—name of Conantum. From Conantum would come my best friends in high school—cool, intellectual girls with divorcing parents, who jeered at my conventional morals and whose only church experience—back in the days when my family still attended Trinity Church—occurred on the unchaperoned coed weekend trips of the Unitarian Church's Liberal Religious Youth. Most of these girls were nonpracticing Jews—there was no synagogue in Concord in those days—and their lack of Protestant disapproval filled me with delight.

But then I had always been drawn to girls from a background less burdened by Puritan moralisms. Even my first best friend in Concord, Janie McClintock—whose non–New England parents were friends of my parents—had attracted me by her wondrous freedom from caring what other people thought. In the sixth grade, when the children everywhere in town were pooled in the Peter Bulkeley School, my friend, Debbie Mancusi, had come from the mill town of West Concord.

Debbie Mancusi had the hoop petticoat (a blow-up tube around the rim) I so envied, and, though from a poorer family than mine, many more new clothes. Debbie was Catholic, and surely privy to plenty of its attendant guilts—

but they were not my guilts, and, in my eyes, anyway, they seemed less burdensome, shed each week at confession. Debbie was pretty, with pale blue eyes and white-blond, flipped hair, a fun girl, a bright girl, a thoroughly nice girl, not mean like her other friends, who wore pancake makeup and formed a group they called "the club," whose members, it was rumored, made out with each other in rehearsal for boys. But Debbie would be separated from me forever when the tracking placements were passed out at the end of sixth grade, only to be glimpsed in the hallways of Emerson Junior High. If the school authorities had put Debbie Mancusi in the Honor Division, where she belonged, maybe she would have had the confidence to stop at third base and not get pregnant her senior year in high school and be forced to drop out and vanish into another state. If I'd been a better person, I would have remained friends with Debbie—as my own children would remain true to their early friends—but the lure of adolescent tribalism had been too strong.

Returning to your hometown as an adult tends to muddy the springs of nostalgia that brought you back. Even the blissful memories of my sixth-grade year could not withstand the reality of who I'd been and who I had become. The unexamined life may not be worth living—a quote often attributed wrongly to Thoreau—but sometimes it looks pretty nice. Living in the scene of my childhood with my Protestant predilection for self-analysis and self-loathing, I became quite the expert of how I'd been a jerk, was still a jerk, and would probably always remain a jerk—just in different ways.

When my high school class had its twenty-fifth reunion, I, who lived in town, couldn't seem to fit it in my schedule. "But it's our twenty-fifth!" said Randy Marr, still living in Concord because his family had never left. Was that his baby sister ringing me out at the Friendly's register with a sullen look? Most of my friends from high school were long gone: they had left New England or, if still in the region, were disinclined to live in their hometown for all the healthy reasons (loath to rake up the past, real estate prices too high, town too preppy) I'd breezed past. Still, I would often run into someone I had known slightly in my youth with whom I had not acquitted myself well: the high school teacher who, after I'd been mean to his son, had (errone-ously) reported me for selling drugs, now retired and chat-tily bagging groceries; the friendly girl who had played first flute in band while I'd miserably faked it on third; the taciturn, stolid woman at the novelties shop who, I the-orized, must be Lee Hill. Lee Hill, who had sat in front of me in the first grade with the same stolidity with which she stands behind the counter today. Lee Hill, who'd been

there the day my rushing urine had roared above the sound
of twenty crayons scribbling, crashing bubblingly into a
yellow puddle beneath my chair. Lee, who'd watched me
lie when I, sticking to my seat, casually told the teacher
that the boy with the speech impediment must have spilled
some water beneath my chair. Lee, now nearing fifty, but
without benefit of a $70-a-month hair-dyeing program.
Sometimes I saw her walking listlessly down Thoreau
Street. Thoreau Street—*Don't name a street after me; name
it after Henry,* said Emerson. But Emerson had been the
lucky one, winding up with his name on a junior high and
a museumed house and the enormous town playground,
where the mingled sounds of basketballs and tennis balls
and baseballs and high-pitched screams will forever bring
back the youth of every Concord child. Meanwhile, Thoreau's name had landed on the most commercial street in
town. Thoreau Street: graceless, nonhistoric, with gas sta-
tions and convenience stores and Dunkin' Donuts (albeit
with a beige sign) and Video Revolution and a train station,
where teenagers smoked God-knows-what and ground
their skateboards on summer nights. When Lee hands
Charlie (in his Concord Country Club baseball cap, dear
God) and me the carefully wrapped, overpriced china
toothbrush holder, do I say then, "Lee, it's Sally Payne!"
the urinating liar who became a bossy teacher's pet and

stepped on everyone's heads to get into Harvard? At least at the reunion I would have met her on a level playing field. But no, I was going away that weekend with friends to New Hampshire.

When I returned from New Hampshire that Sunday, through the door had been pushed a note from Debbie Mancusi. Debbie had made it to the reunion, though she now lived on a houseboat in Sausalito. The note said she "always knew" I'd do "something big like become a writer." She knew this because, although I couldn't seem to find the time to make it to the reunion, I had found quite a bit of time to write a long, long brag about myself to be included in the reunion report. I never wrote her back. I still cry to think of that. Back then I was always crying: my children were teenagers.

CHAPTER TWENTY-ONE

(THE TUNNEL TEENAGERS)

FOR SOME LUCKY REASON, I never romanticize about the boyfriends I didn't marry. But, from time to time, I like to sigh that the Nashawtuc Hill house was the house that got away. I think, with a warming tear, of the late afternoon sun slanting over the sledding hill where my adolescent sons

---

Our third house, photographed from the front yard of our first house: on the left is the old shoe factory where Thoreau borrowed the match and (a century and a half later) my sons partied, while a cop car parked outside, waiting for departing prey.

had showcased their suicidal feats to wide-eyed girls; of the slow-moving river below; of my parents' ill-sourced pride in me; of the comfy kitchen we'd created when Charlie's business had picked up. Unlike the moves before, the move from Nashawtuc Hill had not begun on an optimistic note. I had suffered a few wobbles when Charlie told me that we had to sell the house. But then, shooting through my mortification had been a fresh joy—at the thought of moving.

Despite my parents' disapproval, I soldiered on. Within a week I found a house, no realtor needed—less expensive than the house on Nashawtuc Hill but larger—a long, lovely, low-ceilinged antique Colonial. This find was a warren of white-painted rooms with 250-year-old crooked moldings and working fireplaces. "In the new house, we will have a sewing room!" I proclaimed to nine-year-old Emily, though neither of us sewed.

"Some of our friends actually think you've moved up," my parents said halfheartedly, because a well-to-do friend had once lived there. But after we'd settled in, my parents said, "We don't like this house as much as the house on the hill," piercing my shallow heart. And though I loved the new house as I have loved all my new houses, I still felt so embarrassed by our stumble down the real estate ladder that Charlie had to visit a shrink to try to like me more. "It's not a pretty sight," he said about the aggregate of my bad values when he returned from the appointment, "but at least now I know it's because you have such low self-esteem."

The house was across the street from our first house in Concord. On its stone wall I had waited weepily exuberant for Hunter and Teddy's elementary school bus—I seemed to be reliving my life now at an escalating pace. The pre-Revolutionary house that had brought the Historic Districts Commission swarming to our door across the street eight years before was now ours, and once again I found myself waging battle to change the paint color of my house. But this time there was no craven offering of coffee cake on wedding china; instead I stormed the barricades, appearing before the Historic Commission meeting as hawkish as the women on the dais. So withering was I in my response to their mullion-color suggestions that half the committee timidly abstained when it came to a vote. It wasn't until after I had angrily left what I assumed was my defeat; tried and failed to slam the slow, heavy door of Town Hall behind me; plunked myself into our car and noticed in the rearview mirror the war-paint effect of the lipstick I had viciously slathered on in the dark before confronting the board—that Charlie got a chance to tell me we had won the vote.

The history of my house was moving ever onward. Its

first owner had set the tone in 1773, so outraged about his
tax bill he'd signed an incendiary letter to his king, George
III, that would have had him hanged if the British had
won the Revolutionary War. It was from my house, some
seventy years later, that Thoreau had—I later determined—
borrowed the shoemaker's match that had burnt down
three hundred acres of Concord's woods. Our contributions would be less dramatic. Now outside the house's old
shoe factory room, where my sons slept and partied, a cop
car parked all weekend, waiting for departing prey. "Don't
let anyone leave the house!" I was reduced to calling out
one night when I'd wandered down at two a.m. to find
half the teenagers in Concord in full swing. For it was here
in this snug Colonial, around the corner from Dove Cottage, the first Concord house of the peripatetic Alcotts,
that my children entered the tunnel of teenagehood, and I
entered with them—not with the greatest of grace.

ALL THROUGH Hunter and Teddy's elementary school
years, I had made a point of how imperfect I was, to ease
the pressure they put upon themselves. As it turned out,
nobody had needed to be convinced of my imperfections: it
was their father the boys had been in awe of. "*Daddy?*" I'd
said incredulously, then proceeded to tell stories about

their father's many imperfections: the Cs in school, how once he'd drunkenly crashed his family's car into a stone wall, how he'd been thrown into jail for a night in college, etc., etc. I continued to tell these stories well into the middle school years—they were very popular with both boys (I noticed the topic seemed naturally to crop up when Charlie was on a business trip)—explaining how these very imperfections made their father lovable.

Then came my sons' first summer in the new old house on Wood Street, before their ninth and eighth grades, when Hunter and Teddy just wanted to "relax." "You always put so much pressure on us to get good grades!" I was told. I who had never raised my voice was told, "You're always yelling at me." I who had always praised was told, "You're always so critical." Suddenly, I wondered if they were right. And so, operating on the same hope-springs-eternal theory my mother had—that we trusted our teenage children at the exact moment in their lives when they no longer trusted themselves—I suspended the rules that had guided their everyday lives. The boys—who in years past would have been shocked to be served dessert that had not been preceded by fruit ("Six grapes, please!" the neighborhood friend whose family had no rules had happily cried out)— suddenly had no bedtimes, no planned summer activities, no need even to tell me where they were going. "Use your own judgment," I counseled, as my own mother had counseled me as a teenager—*before I'd driven stoned to the airport!* should have been one of several thoughts that sprang to mind. But instead I thought how sweet to see the guilty pleasure my sons took, as if they were being wild, when they stayed up all night with their friends watching television and baking trays of brownies at three a.m. and going off in high spirits to swim at Walden Pond at the break of day.

"You mean they're not drinking or smoking pot?" the other mothers asked in amazement. I could only shake my head—an atom bomb would not have dislodged me from my belief that my teenagers were different from all teenagers who had ever lived. Even when one summer evening a sweet little friend of Emily's, who was the daughter of an assistant minister, discovered a Tupperware container which smelled funny (*like bourbon,* I concluded), I held on, summoning my sons from their friends' houses in a serious but not an angry voice. For though they were innocent, the fact of another teenager drinking alcohol had to be treated as a somber affair.

Still, when Hunter and Teddy arrived, I could not help but smile to see them whispering to each other. The boys had not been friends since Hunter had hit third grade and had had to be put on a separate soccer team from Teddy, because he'd been afraid that Teddy would score more goals. After this, had begun (until middle school) Charlie's and my long talks with the boys every night before bed, each parent taking a different son, so that each brother could express—in a safe atmosphere—how much he hated the other one's guts. The listening parent would feign sympathy, careful not to utter one word in the absent child's defense. This had been my invention, as most of the "parenting" ideas had been. Charlie's were more along the lines of "Don't ask, don't tell." "What do you think we should do about Teddy?" I'd asked Hunter one night after Teddy had taken his favorite shirt. "I think we should kill him," Hunter had said.

But now I saw my boys united again. Yes, they admitted ruefully, some kid no one knew *had* shown up one night with alcohol in the Tupperware. I would not ask them to name names, I said, nor would I punish them for something they did not do, but I would ask them, man to man, to promise to inform me if anyone ever entered the house with liquor again. "Thank you for your honesty," I said, dismissing them with a hug, and then sighing as I leaned back into the sofa, waiting to hear the jangle of the front door closing—sleigh bells attached to keep things merry—before heading to the liquor cabinet myself. Suddenly it seemed a bit unseemly to pour myself a Stoli and tonic.

The next afternoon, a phone call from a Cambridge

policeman informed me, with the force necessary to convince, that Hunter had not been at a Shakespearean play in Boston with his friends, as I had huffily maintained, but on the banks of the Charles River, smoking a joint and drinking vodka out of a chocolate drink.

And then it all came out—well, some of it, anyway. How in middle school Hunter and Teddy had discovered an old joint of Charlie's on the mantel, and *did we know how disillusioning it was to learn your father smoked pot as a* grownup? *Did we know,* they continued, *that they often hear my friend Kerry and me laughing and can tell that we are drunk? No, no,* I tried to defend myself, *Kerry doesn't even drink, we were just having a good time,* but then I remembered, God help me, that there *had* been times in the happy past when I had had a few drinks or so with friends. And I realized with chill certainty that that happy past was now over. *Whatever happened to going out and getting drunk?* Nathaniel Hawthorne had lamented in his late fifties. The answer is: you had teenagers.

"But you and Daddy did it," the boys cried out, as Charlie and I scrambled to moralize about teenage drinking, "and you *drove.*" Now all my endearing stories about Charlie were brought into evidence. "'Drinking and smoking will obscure the real teenage experience,'" I tried weakly, dredging up repressed memories from the fifth-grade DARE

program, when we parents had bitten our tongues instead
of saying, "Don't make that a promise!" as our children,
one by one, had pledged at the podium that they would
never, ever smoke a cigarette or have an alcoholic drink.
"Look at your uncle Hunter," I tried next, "who smoked
pot as a teenager and dropped out of college after a week!"
"But he has the best life ever!" said Teddy and Hunter, for
it *would* be that uncle who had made so much money he
could write songs in his house by the sea with a beautiful
wife, and not need to work.

Our moralizing seemed only to solidify Hunter's suspi-
cion that he was on the side of the damned. In one week,
three containers of Mace (for what purpose I dared not
ask), charged on my Visa, arrived in the mail for Hunter;
marijuana was found growing in his bathroom; and one
night Hunter did not return home from a party until eight
in the morning. "Don't worry, he'll be home," Charlie had
said at one a.m., as he drifted off to a sleep that would not
continue quite as long as he had prophesied.

My mind became so scrambled with what to think and
what to say, and whether Hunter would live through another weekend, that I could do only what my besieged
mother had done: turn to the experts. I found a shrink who
specialized in teenagers and dragged Charlie with me, returning to tell Hunter (while trying to believe it myself)

that lying, drinking, smoking, shoplifting, staying out all night—were not *moral* issues but *safety* issues. *Do your drinking at home*, was what it amounted to, though not so baldly stated, and Hunter, so literal, seeking sanction even for his disobedience, said, "I know I'm not supposed to drink, but if I do, where do I get the liquor?" "Steal it from me," I answered, wondering if I meant it.

At my request, the shrink for teenagers (to which neither of my teenagers would go) gave us our own set of parental rules. We were never to leave the house for more than three hours, until the kids turned twenty-one, for one; and, for another, we were (pretty much) to stop drinking ourselves, except mildly on our short evenings out, when Charlie would sneak to the car two watery cocktails to sip on the way to the movies. One such night, as we drove off down Thoreau Street, we caught sight of Teddy walking home with his skateboard and waved gaily for him to jump into the car so we could give him a ride—only to remember, as Teddy plopped into the backseat, the two bubbling gin and tonics with limes in our cup holders. "Don't worry," Teddy said with a little smirk, "I won't tell Hunter."

TEDDY HAD possibly escaped some of the grinding guilt of his older brother. Certainly as a young child he had seemed less burdened. One Christmas, after six-year-old Hunter had given us his carefully handmade Christmas card, Teddy had cried piteously how he wished he'd given us a homemade Christmas card too! "Well, Teddy," I'd said brightly, "how about that half-finished card in your backpack?" "Nah," Teddy had shrugged and run out to play.

When Teddy began to turn from us in middle school, his lightheartedness had sometimes leaked out in our presence. "I'm trying to surprise myself," he confided one afternoon, when I found him lying expectantly on the living room sofa, as the smell of the apple (or was it *raspberry*??) turnover he was baking wafted in from the kitchen.

Even in high school, Teddy seemed happy, except for the brief moments he happened to be in the same room with his mother. "You know, I'm the only one of my friends who doesn't have a police record," he might mention in passing, so that I didn't know whether to be glad he didn't have a record, or worried that he had friends who did. Sometimes, though, he would make an inviting remark like, "I like my social studies teacher a lot," fleeing the kitchen before I had a chance to kill the conversation with, "Oh, really, in what way?" Often I became so excited when he actually spoke to me that I would interrupt him by finishing his sentences. "Well, I guess I don't need to tell you what I was going to say," Teddy would shrug, causing me once to cry out (to the blankest of responses), "I under-stand completely! I hate me too!"

Every afternoon at two fifteen, I would anxiously await the hiss of Teddy's high school bus, perching myself at the top of the stairs so that my feigned casual descent would happen to coincide with Teddy's opening of the refrigerator door. Coming down, I would wonder what I could say to prepare the way for a lively give-and-take between mother and son. Surely I could come up with something more imaginative than "How was school?" The magazines at the hairdresser's suggested asking more specific questions like, "How was gym?" to show a more informed interest, but I had found these questions equally rhetorical. Knowing I'd be allowed one sentence if I was lucky, I would try every time to think of the exact right thing to say to reach my son as he vanished behind the opened refrigerator door—but always, always, *always* I would blurt out the futile conversation killer, "So, how was school today?" "Good," Teddy would answer as he brushed past me.

But in the next room, I would hear him whistling away, glad—just possibly—that his mother was home.

CHAPTER TWENTY-TWO

WRITING ABOUT YOUR FAMILY

PAINTING HAS ALWAYS BEEN considered a feminine art in the leisure class. "Everyone's an artist in Concord," my mother's friend Mrs. Potter said recently as we tried in vain to catch the attention of several Concord widows in their late eighties rapt in a four-hour painting class, "except, of course, for your poor mother." Painting was safe. It was ladylike. You were never going to make a living at it. (Those who do, if they exist, immediately become unsafe.) You

Once Thoreau's country store, and later mine.

could paint, looking fresh and pretty with a ribbon around your head; you could paint as your children played or on holiday with your husband. And it is pretty hard to spill the family secrets in a watercolor of the Ponte Vecchio.

But writing books, even for my mother's generation, still had a tinge of the masculine, smacking too much of public exposure and overeducation and grubby hands and overexcited talk at the dinner table. (Unless of course the writing brought you fame. "My favorite girl!" my father once greeted Doris Kearns Goodwin, Concord's most beloved resident, as the three women most suitable for the honorific—my mother, Emily, and I—looked on.) Even the much admired American architecture books Janie McClintock published had their downside, since she had to rise at five a.m. to write them before tending to her children and leaving for her full-time job. Though surely proud of Janie's resourcefulness, her mother had sighed nevertheless as she stood in my front hall, "I do wish Janie cared more about her house."

In the early 1990s, my mother and her friends began to brace themselves for the semi-autobiographical novels to come from their college-educated daughters. News came of one such novel splashing upon the scene, written by the daughter of a friend of my mother's and glowingly reviewed—its title, the ill-boding *Swallow Hard*. Another friend gave my mother cocktail napkins that said, "Don't spank them. They'll only write about it later."

Instead of talking honestly to my mother, I wrote books filled with surprises. I wanted her to say, *Aren't you funny about me*, and *That's the opposite of what I think, and yet— I agree!*, and *Why do you think you're such a bad person— you're not!* Instead, I saw her flinching at the exposure my books brought. How could I blame her when I myself got more migraines publishing my books than writing them? ("What's the good part about writing again?" Charlie would ask, driving me to the ER.) My mother was so anxious about what other people thought, she couldn't help sometimes throwing me to the dogs: dutifully leaving on my front hall table the panning, never-expecting-to-be-published review her old friend took upon herself to write about my novel to be expressly delivered to me by my mother.

But a part of her was proud that I had braved the mul-titudes, that I had stuck to it, in the try-hard New England way. She allowed me to publish anything about herself, even about money; she came to my readings and gave me a party; she wrote me the same sanctioning letter with the exact same words about each book, no matter how much pain the book had given her ("It is a good book, and well-written").

When she died, I thought I'd killed her.

I MAY HAVE felt guilty about what I'd written, but Louisa Alcott, as a woman of her time, felt guilty that she wrote at all. Even Sophia Hawthorne, an artist herself (but, safely, a painter), agreed with her husband, who wrote: "I wish [women] were forbidden to write, on pain of having their faces deeply scarified with an oyster-shell."

Writing about her family had never been Louisa's plan. *Hospital Sketches*—written after Louisa had returned from nursing Civil War soldiers, half dead at age thirty from typhoid and poisoned by the mercury "cure"—had been well received and praised by Emerson. Buoyed, she had plunged back to work on her true love, *Moods*, an adult novel, its hero based on Thoreau. Louisa had always been careful not to compare herself to the exalted men of her youth, but with *Moods*, "genius burned so fiercely" she allowed herself to hope. Not for long. In his brutal review of *Moods*—which he called *Dumps*—twenty-something Henry James wrote the "two most striking facts . . . are the author's ignorance of human nature and her self-confidence in spite of this ignorance." (Or put a triter way, *Write about what you know*.)

With her ambition to be an adult novelist crushed; feeling "jailed" after a trip abroad to be stuck in "boring" Concord, where Marmee was sick and getting sicker— Louisa resigned herself at age thirty-five to writing *Little Women*. The Alcotts—surprise, surprise—were in debt.

The publisher had told Bronson he thought a girls' book would sell, and Bronson, magnanimous as always when it came to offering up the efforts of others, had signed his daughter up. So with a heavy sigh, Louisa had set about writing a syrupy syllogism based on her father's fantasy about his family's life, churning out Part One of *Little Women* in three months, the first draft the only draft. Even the title came from Bronson's own condescending hope that his daughters would become accepting, passive receptacles of his wisdom.

"Write about what you know!" is the famous advice to writers, and one that nobody can ever say I have not taken to heart. ("Shall I just give up and keep writing about myself on and on forever?" I recently asked an editor as she slashed away all the historical writing I'd spent years researching. "Yep," she said.) With *Little Women*, Louisa took what she knew—her family—and transformed it. She deleted all the bad parts and threw a pound of sugar at the rest. There was no starving at a wacky Utopia, no moving twenty times, no public debacles or talk of free love. The father in the novel—blessedly absent most of the time—loses his money not by ruining the family with crazy profligacy, but by lending it generously to a friend; the novel's Marmee, instead of being a wreck, is the calm pillar of wisdom. Agoraphobic "Beth" is divine; "Meg" (Anna) blissfully leaves home for love—not, as in reality, to get away from all the fighting; "Jo" (Louisa) is an outgoing tomboy, not a miserable recluse. The only character who seems to have escaped the sugar load is the selfish "Amy" (May)—the sister I had chosen to identify with, so embarrassingly, in my youth.

To Louisa and her publisher's surprise, Part One of *Little Women* sold extremely well. Nothing is so inspiring for the self-loather as the praise and approval of others. Emerson criticized Thoreau (in his eulogy no less) for picking berries instead of writing, but Thoreau was always writing—it was self-doubt that impeded his publishing more. Louisa was charged with success as she wrote Part Two—"so full of my work I can't stop to eat or sleep." Part One had been ground out at Orchard House in the nest of the demanding family; Part Two was written in a rented room in Boston, away from the home she was reinventing. Her irritation lifted, Louisa's ten-year-old pain about Beth's death broke through the platitudes and became her inspiration.

Finishing in less than two months, she collapsed into cough and chills; she was still feeling low when Part Two was published, but "the family seems so panic-stricken and helpless when I break down, that I try to keep the mill going."

The mill was a success beyond anyone's dreams. By August, Louisa had sold twenty-three thousand copies, and by January she'd received royalties of $8,500 and paid off all the family's debts. Beth had died in 1858, but it wasn't until *Little Women* was published in 1868 that Louisa could pay off the doctor "—[A]nd now I feel as if I could die in peace," she wrote. Except that she couldn't ever find peace. Her constant state of guilt could only be relieved by constant remunerative work; most journal entries contained exact amounts of money earned. When Anna's husband died in 1870, Louisa cut short a pleasure trip to Europe, racing home to write *Little Men* to support Anna and her sons, though Anna's husband had left them plenty to live on.

Louisa had been determined to win fame since she was a girl. But when she became famous, she begged to be left alone. The well of bitterness in Marmee's heart against the society she had been born into and fallen beneath had been transferred to her daughters and made them unfit for other homes. Louisa would have wished away her fame except that with the fame came the money to take care of the ailing Marmee. About Marmee, Louisa had no conflicting thoughts, and so Marmee's death, which came nine years after *Little Women* was published, though deeply sad, was bearable.

But the death two years later of Louisa's youngest sister, May—who as the mercenary "Amy" is the only unredeemable family member in *Little Women*—was unbearable. Louisa felt a deep guilt about her brutally honest, unflattering portrayal of the sister she'd envied in real life. And when May died, Louisa thought she'd killed her.

CHAPTER TWENTY-THREE

HOMESICK III

FOR SOMEONE so embarrassingly homesick, it is odd that I have moved so many times. Sometimes when I am stupidly longing for home when off on a great vacation with my husband and children, I forget for a moment which home I am being homesick for. "Don't move too much or your children won't have memories," my mother cautioned many years ago. Perhaps this is why Emily, even as a young teen-

---

Hawthorne, after three honeymoon years at The Old Manse, would long for Concord in the nearly two decades he was forced to be away.

ager, would spend ecstatic weekends making scrapbooks dating back to preschool, and take *The House at Pooh Corner* to bed—trying to hold on.

I don't know whether adult homesickness is genetic, or a product of an unsettled childhood; whether it's a neurosis, a liability, or the tool that makes a writer; or whether it can be caused by the qualities of an actual place. But whatever the makeup of adult homesickness, the Concord Authors and their families seemed to have been afflicted with it also. Most of them were moved constantly in their youth by parents who were scrambling for jobs and money; none of them was born in Concord (except for Thoreau, removed at two months of age), and yet all of them went to considerable difficulty to make it home. The Alcotts, despite humiliation in a self-righteous town, kept moving away and bouncing back. Hawthorne, after a mere three years' residence in his late thirties, would long for Concord in the two decades he was forced to be away, and finally return to end his days here. Emerson, who had remarked that he had just happened to pick Concord to settle in, was being disingenuous. His grandparents had watched the Revolution commence in the backyard of their Concord house, The Old Manse, and Emerson's few idyllic summers as a boy had been spent there. And, certainly, no one was more tied to Concord than Henry Thoreau, who could not travel to another state without a clutch of the throat—even the view from the top of a Maine mountain was too vast.

Despite the miseries of their childhood, three of the Alcott daughters as adults were homesick whenever they were away, dysfunctionally so. Beth never left home, even to go to school. Anna, after a stab at independence, moved her obliging husband and two kids back in with her parents. Even Louisa, the women's advocate, ran from Concord and her all-consuming parents in order to write, but she always returned to them, for they were her identity. Just as my parents had been mine, long after they should have been.

But the youngest Alcott, May ("Amy"), wasn't as plagued by homesickness as the rest of us. Born after the stillbirth of a brother, she had been cherished as an infant rather than examined as a developing soul. Or possibly, she had simply been born with the gift for happiness—like my father, or my eldest brother, Billy, less crippled than the rest of my family by worthless guilt. In any case, May had left the worrying about family collapse to her sisters, and lobbied her exhausted parents successfully for art lessons and finery. Louisa: "[A]lways seems to feel the moment she is having a good time that she is doing wrong . . ." said Anna. But the baby, May, had been as joyous as their indomitable father.

And though Louisa could not help resenting her youngest sister's liberty from guilt and want, she also admired it, and worked hard to ensure it. May went off to Europe (financed by Louisa) and wore fashionable Parisian clothes and sent home braggy, competitive letters about her success as a painter—"proof that Lu does not monopolize all the Alcott talent. Ha! ha! sister. . . ." No trip home for May when Marmee lay dying—just an engagement following her mother's death to a good-looking man fifteen years younger, who serenaded her with a violin and lavished upon her all the thoughtful attentions Marmee and Louisa and most New England mothers and daughters had never dreamed of, and perhaps would have been horrified to receive. May wrote crowing letters about her wonderful, sensuously luxurious married life: of delightful fabrics and silverware and lunch parties and boat rides and love in a country house outside Paris. If Louisa only knew how nice life could be, she gushed.

When May died four weeks after delivering a baby girl, Louisa was consumed with guilt. If only she could have made it to Europe, she ruminated, somehow she might have saved her. May's death Louisa deemed as the worst thing ever to happen to her—to have seen "someone so high brought so low." But the true agony of May's death for Louisa went still deeper, I think. Subconsciously Louisa felt that her jealousy—made so public in the indictment of

Amy in *Little Women*—had led to May's death. Louisa had had a presentiment that her sister would die, and so had her sister.

"May felt a foreboding," Louisa wrote, "and had left all ready in case she died." When her dead sister's things arrived on Louisa's doorstep, Louisa wrote, "Of all the trials in my life I never felt any as keenly as this."

But maybe May had been unable completely to escape guilt herself. Perhaps May felt as my mother felt, and as I and so many other New Englanders irrationally feel—that great happiness can only be followed by punishment. For May had tempted the fates. May had known it was dangerous to become pregnant at forty and she had faced the risk, so guilty at her happiness that she was willing to let God take it away. Not only had she packed up all her trunks and diaries while pregnant, she had chosen her gravesite. With a heady thrill, she had written Louisa ecstatically, saying, that if she died in childbirth she didn't care, it had all been worth it. She'd been so happy, not to be in Concord.

CHAPTER TWENTY-FOUR

DEATH AND MOTHERHOOD I

MOST OF THE NARCISSISTS I know lead long and happy lives, and Bronson Alcott was no exception. Even after a massive stroke felled him in 1882 in his early eighties, he managed to keep the party going for the six-year grace period that followed. Settled in a sunny study in the town he loved, nursed by daughters, surrounded by his books

---

Bronson perfected his state of "beingness" next to the parlor where Thoreau had expired, twenty years earlier, struggling to finish The Maine Woods.

and busts, he spent his twilight years rereading the fifty volumes of journals which he believed would light up the world after he had left it. No man would ever die more graciously certain of a genius absent in the work he left behind.

But perhaps there is a God, or at least a Protestant Protector, because I have yet to see that true narcissists leave much behind in accomplishment. What writer can succeed who can't see beyond himself, or even within himself? I know of no one, not his friends or biographers then or now, who asks you to read a word that Bronson wrote. Even Odell Shepard, who won a Pulitzer Prize in 1938 for his biography of Bronson, was at a loss to name Bronson's contribution to the world. Did seventy years of conversation count? Shepard guessed not, weakly concluding that Bronson could be credited for providing Louisa with the cozy, happy family life she portrayed in *Little Women*. All I can say to that is, my goodness. My goodness.

If you can't say something nice about someone, don't say anything at all is a principle that has fueled the legacy of guilt and ruined the writing of many a WASP. Surely the near-absence of the father in *Little Women* is the most powerful proof of Louisa's mixed feelings. She had been taught to love her father through her mother's stubborn devotion, but respect him she could not. Even in fiction, she could not credit Bronson for family happiness. But to the living we owe respect, and to the dead, well, truth is the plank I have held on to in the Protestant storm. So let me release Louisa from her constraints by saying that Bronson's contribution to the world was that he gave his daughter her motive for living—to right the wrongs he had done her mother—and by so doing drove her to write the girls' book she didn't want to write. To pay all debts and take care of her mother—and, by extension, her family—was Louisa's mantra, and the only justification for her writing, which sometimes gave her a guilty pleasure.

My mother had been determined not to be a "burden" on her children from the beginning and had moved into assisted living before she needed it. But the moody Marmee had looked to moody Louisa as soul mate and helpmeet since she was a little girl. And so, though the family breadwinner and often very ill herself, Louisa had nursed Marmee through the decade of her decline. On her last day, Marmee said she was very happy to die, and then drifted into a reverie of being a little girl again, calling Louisa "Mother."

But mothering one's mother is a travesty of motherhood. It was only when Louisa became a real mother a few years later—when she adopted May's baby—that she learned what life could be.

After her mother died, Louisa's conflicting emotions

about Bronson mellowed into simple affection. Her father no longer disapproved of her—and not enough can be said of the power of that. (Even today, several years after their death, I taste the nectar of my parents grown too old to disapprove, happy, happy just to hear my voice over the phone. "Darling!" my mother would say whenever she picked up.) Bronson was, in fact, proud of his daughter in the good old American way. I mean, let's be honest here—all one's worry about who your children will become and what they will contribute to the world would be swept away in an instant if they started making a ton of money. Bronson not only approved of Louisa's money, he managed it for her. With good old lucre, Louisa had finally won over the above-money, male chauvinist Bronson, whose model of the perfect companion for himself neither Louisa nor her mother had ever approached. (Beth came closest, but then Beth couldn't have provided him with a single apple.)

For twenty years, Louisa had put up with the crumbling money pit that was Orchard House—spring-cleaning it, cooking in it, nursing in it. She had not done it for Bronson. The moment her mother began to die, Louisa ditched the home Bronson had labored so lovingly on and moved the family into the Thoreau house on Main Street, where the last Thoreau (the youngest sister) had recently died. There in the study built expressly for him by Louisa, Bronson perfected his state of "beingness," next to the room where Thoreau had expired twenty years before (and forty-four years younger), struggling to finish *The Maine Woods*. For the next three years, Bronson went great guns, though May died and Emerson lay dying, vowing to live to be a hundred. Even after the stroke hit, Bronson revived, recovering his speech and also, according to some, a full head of hair over his bald pate. In the meantime, though throbbing with headache, dizziness, vertigo, stomach pains, and aching limbs, Louisa continued taking care of everyone in the family, until she became too sick. Then she exiled herself to a nursing home in Dorchester, where she struggled to write an hour a day. As opposed to Thoreau who had chosen to die in his mother's parlor, Louisa seemed loath to let her family care for her. Louisa was the true recluse—not Thoreau, the famous one, who had once hosted thirty people in his tiny cabin at Walden (the secret to entertaining, he rather brilliantly advised, was never to mention "dinner").

But like Thoreau, Louisa tried to keep writing till the end. Even her last year, 1888, she found her "head full of a story that won't let me alone." In January of that year, she wrote that she, aged fifty-five, "had no more strength than a baby . . . I look about 70—grey & wrinkled & bent & lame." The first of March, she dragged herself to visit her father and found him so blissful she wondered what he was thinking. "Going *up*," Bronson confided. "Come with me." Even in this, she would oblige, catching a chill after a visit and dying two days after Bronson. She was buried in Sleepy Hollow, laid at the feet of her family, as if in death as in life she would be its doormat.

BUT DO NOT CRY for Louisa, and not because she left *Little Women* behind. *Little Women* is a great book for girls and it was recognized as such while Louisa lived. And if Louisa scorned her writing for children, still she felt pride in the effect it had on her audience. Most important for Louisa, *Little Women* and the books it spawned gave her money for Marmee and the rest of her family. Louisa succeeded in her stated aim to take care of her mother. But she never succeeded in the aim she dared not speak aloud—to write a great adult book (in the eyes of anyone but her mother, who read *Moods* twenty times).

Louisa's motive for living might have died along with Marmee and May, who had both done her the great service of needing her in a way that the self-gratifying Bronson and the contented Anna had not. But, fortunately for Louisa, May still needed Louisa after death. Or put another way, May finally gave her sister something back.

Nine months after May's death, her daughter, Lulu, arrived in America, bequeathed to her aunt, now guardian. Louisa wrote, "[A] little yellow-haired thing in white . . . came to me saying 'Marmar' in a wistful way and nestling close as if she had found her own people and home at last, as she had,— thank Heaven! . . . She always comes to me, and seems to have decided that I am really 'Marmar.'" At age forty-eight, Louisa had suddenly became a mother. While holding Lulu, she thought that "even death had its compensations" and "I see now why I lived,— to care for May's child and not leave Anna all alone." When Bronson had his stroke, Lulu "ran to meet me, rosy and gay, and I felt as if I could bear anything with this little sunbeam to light up the world for me."

No wonder it took Louisa more than four years to write her last book, instead of a couple of months. She worried, with the rest of us, about all the little domestic matters of motherhood. The last seven years of her life, Louisa showered upon Lulu—"my one joy"—all the love Marmee had showered upon her. And like Marmee, Louisa shied away from discipline, so much so that Lulu would sometimes beg for it. Lulu was a handful, as Louisa herself had been. One time after the little girl had urged Louisa to spank her, Louisa wrote, "She proudly says, 'Do it, do it!' and when it is done is heartbroken at the idea of Aunt Wee-wee's giving her pain. . . . Love is better; but also endless patience."

Unlike Marmee, Louisa was able to buy her "daughter" everything, even a house by the ocean where Lulu is "wild for joy and freedom." And if her writing suffered, Louisa shrugged it off, too busy arranging cakes and presents for Lulu's birthday. There was no real worry about spoiling Lulu with money, as there had been in my parents' generation, more of a determination (as in mine) to shower her child with it. Nor did suddenly having money make Louisa more frugal, as it had my mother—Louisa spent freely, letting her father (reveling in his new role as capitalist) do the investing.

Those who feel less live longer, or so it seems to me. And so in the end, I pose an ageless question, as purposeless as childhood's *would you rather be deaf or blind?*: Would one rather have been Bronson or Louisa? Bronson, who had either remained serene in the storm or been the storm itself; Bronson, cared for by all, who lived thirty years longer than his daughter. Or depressive Louisa, who had felt sick nearly every day of her life after age thirty; Louisa, who had worked obsessively to her death, but whose suffering was illuminated by deep, joyous flashes from the happiness she created for others. Like my mother, battling the Furies but getting supper on the table by seven.

Louisa had shared a birthday with her father, and often she had complained in her journal that she'd never had a good one. Year after year, she'd gloomily noted, the day had passed with no presents for Louisa.

But though Louisa would spend her last birthday prostrate in a nursing home, it would nevertheless be her happiest birthday ever. She wrote, "I had such a jolly birthday that I had to rest after it. . . . I had 40 gifts in all." Perhaps, like her mother, all she asked for was a little recognition. Lying in this anonymous place, this suffering woman, who had longed for death since she was a teenager, seemed to feel a deep euphoric peace as she rested, as if already in heaven, listening to the exuberant child she had raised and would leave behind: "& I heard Lulu rush up, then, in the bed room she stopped & came in so quietly, looking so pale & excited I hardly knew her for my tornado."

CHAPTER TWENTY-FIVE

DEATH AND
MOTHERHOOD II

WHEN I WAS GROWING UP, the nearest anyone in Concord came to being considered "nouveau riche" was Mr. Montgomery. Mr. Montgomery came from the same background as my parents and their friends, but he had had the tackiness to earn a salary so huge, it got reported in a national magazine as the highest in the country. When the Mont-

---

*The Hartwell Tavern, on the road the
British took to Concord.*

gomerys bought a large white house on Main Street, many jokes were made about the uniformed maid and cook and the teenage daughters wearing minks to Trinity Church. Humorous deprecating remarks were made about the Montgomerys' glorious old house. "All I know," joked Mr. Glowers, "is that *I* don't have heating pipes running through my living room." Pity was expressed for little Haley Montgomery (later a financier and TV personality), who answered the door on Halloween in a velvet dress and couldn't wait to visit our house, where she was allowed to feed the dog. In Concord of the 1950s and 1960s, no matter how deep your trust funds ran, you did not hire anyone other than the once-a-week cleaning lady, for whom you made lunch (and with whom you ate it).

But today—the new money has splashed upon the scene not with uniformed maids, but burgeoning "restorations," built onto (and sometimes on top of) vetted houses near the historic center. Concord has been discovered again, but this time the old Protestants are the Indians dying out, and the new settlers the stronger breed, less guilty about their money because they have actually earned it—a step forward, surely, a breath of fresh air, I used to think, until slowly and steadily the numbers began to overwhelm me. Once I had chuckled at the four-bay garages of the erupting developments, but now the new rich are plundering the old neighborhoods and laying waste to the town's old stores. The store where Emily had bought a neon yoyo for $6 is now a boutique selling a nice top to teenagers for $300. As my mother had sniffed twenty years ago, I sniff today, "Concord is just not the same anymore." Suddenly I yearn for the shabby millionaires refilling their cups at Dunkin' Donuts to save 83¢. "Bring back the trust-funded people, they're so much nicer!" my friend who worked at Mail Boxes Etc. cries out. For the new money breeds arrogance, while the old money breeds anxious-to-please guilt, the great undervalued neurosis. The old WASPs are happy to be relegated to the end of the line, they welcome it.

When I think of the migraines I experienced trying to get the approval of my mother's friends! It turns out I didn't need the old girls' approval, because they were on their way out, their beautiful shabby houses soon to be bulldozed over, rocketing their inhabitants to condos in West Concord, until their final move to Sleepy Hollow. And I, the new old girl, am next in line for extinction. Meanwhile the new new girls skip to the head of the line. Without even a pretense of owning a copy of *Walden*, they serve on Concord museum boards, penning personal thank-you notes to me, whom they have never met and never wish to meet, for my grimy little contributions. For just as books do furnish a room, our Concord authors continue to furnish this town.

My parents were old money after the money was long gone. They clung to their sense of class, not because they didn't want equality for all—few were more liberal in view than they—but because it was their identity. Maybe it was a deeply flawed identity, but it was better than no identity. And so too has my identity been a poor one—based on a silly family pride that has not deserved itself for many generations, on raising my children in houses we can't afford, on having my parents at hand to monitor my successes and failures. And yet as I lose, one by one, these factors of my fatuous identity, still I miss them, because without them I am lost.

GEORGE SANTAYANA, the philosopher, understood the New England Puritan better than anyone I have ever read, and it is no wonder that Richard D. Richardson, Jr., quotes him in his biography of Emerson: "Everything in nature is lyrical in its ideal essence, tragic in its fate, and comic in its existence." I quote him now to cloak my embarrassment of the miracle that befell me in 2001: a miracle so silly it befit the wrenching comedy that was my parents and I. After all the shenanigans I had put them through, seeking their approval, I finally won their unqualified acceptance, but for the wrong reason. I won it not for writing books, not for my torturing, overcompensating generosity (the reverse side of cheapness), and not because any of us had risen above our neuroses in recognition of the tenacity of our primal relationship. No, I was redeemed in May of 2001 when I was elected to—The Ladies Four O'Clock Club, an ancient Concord institution, whose very name I must disguise.

The Ladies Four O'Clock Club! How can I explain to the real world, or even to my world, about—The Ladies Four O'Clock Club, with its $5 annual dues, which its treasurer dunned you for mercilessly at the year's first meeting; The Ladies Four O'Clock Club, which carefully kept its existence secret to spare the feelings of the nonelected; The Ladies Four O'Clock Club, whose thirty Elect members (someone had to die before a new member was elected, not an impossibility with the average age hovering at seventy) met the first Thursday of each month for *purely social reasons*. That meant—no gardening or painting or volunteer work please!—but simply time to relax together without the age-old obligations of their busy Concord activities. The Ladies Four O'Clock Club, filled to the brim with the brisk, no-nonsense Protestant women I feared most in the world. And now I had been asked to join their ranks.

When my mother called with the news, there had been

awe in her voice and in my father's silence as he listened on the extension. Women all over town have been up for election multiple times and *never* been invited to join The Ladies Four O'Clock Club, I was informed in tremulous voice. Twenty years ago, Muddy West, upon receiving her invitation to join, had made the fatal mistake of declining because she was too busy that spring. "Well," my mother said, "*she* was never asked again." My mother herself had not been elected until she was seventy years of age. It had been the crowning achievement of her life.

But in my mother's voice there had also been fear. Perhaps she understood me well enough to know that joining The Ladies Four O'Clock Club was the last thing in the world I would want to do. Surely, but not certainly, she had finally gleaned something of who her daughter was, but she could not take the risk of giving me the opportunity of saying no. Of all the many things I had denied her—no lunches because I worked; no dinner parties to meet interesting couples my age; no going to the Unitarian Church to nod away one's guilty affluence in liberal causes—for her, the chance that I would turn down this invitation was a terror greater than the sum of all the other disappointments I'd inflicted. But my mother had just been diagnosed with a bad heart. When I said yes, my parents said, "We've never been so proud of you in all our lives." Two months later, my mother was dead.

ONE OF MY MOTHER'S most fervent beliefs was that the high divorce rate of modern times sprang from a blasphemous disregard for the evening meal. "Do you sit down to dinner together every night?" she had asked her divorcing sons in a low voice as if she were inquiring about their sex lives. That my brothers' wives worked was not factored in, despite the fact that the one time my mother had the semblance of a job—jury duty for two weeks—she'd used her per diem to take my father to a restaurant every night.

When I think of the tumult of our family's sit-down dinners growing up—with me clomping to the table in my father's open-buckled galoshes because I wasn't allowed to dine barefoot; with Johnny filling us in on why short girls were a better fit in bed; with my brother Hunter squashing his Camel cigarette in his bowl of brown rice; with Billy stomping away after my father objected to him cleaning his plate in thirty seconds like a convict—I cannot decide if my mother was very wrong, or very right. Perhaps biting the hand that fed us every night was what saw my brothers and me through. Certainly it saw my mother through. Now that I've had teenagers and have obsessed late into the night about what to tell them, I envy my mother in the desperate predawn being able to say to herself with a calming conviction: "Roast beef, Minute Rice, and *broccoli*."

Much of my mother's life centered, like Lidian Emerson's, around the moral imperative of meals. Not to say my mother's meals were gourmet, or even particularly fresh, even after she'd had time on her hands. "I'll bring the sweet potatoes!" my mother insisted when coming to my house one Thanksgiving, only to show up with three cans of yams and a bag of marshmallows. Even after we grew up and there was no need to prepare three squares a day, the stress, fueled by anxious love and self-doubt, remained. There was so much discussion of when and where and what we were going to eat, that even visiting my parents for a night up at their summer cabin in New Hampshire became as fraught as a state visit.

My mother's meal-centered traumas had only seemed to increase after the rationale for them disappeared. So it is somehow fitting that a falling mayonnaise jar from a jam-packed refrigerator was what broke my mother's toe and eventually did her in. Or so, a bit incredibly, the doctor said a year and a half after the jar had fallen, when they opened her up and found her heart so clogged up from the lack of exercise due to her broken toe, that she died before her operation could begin.

The operation had been elective. "You should be proud of your mother, she was determined to have a better quality of life," her young doctor said minutes after she'd died. In fact, as my mother's three heart doctors—each handsomer than the last—came to see us that morning, I could see why my mother had risen so nobly to the challenge. The 10 percent risk of death (which in my experience generally translates to 100 percent) had been waved off by my mother with the same valiant, unfounded optimism that had taken her through life, solving some problems while creating more. And just as the WASPs don't have funerals (because, I suppose, that might encourage whining) but memorials "celebrating the life of the dead," so my mother's looming operation had been an occasion for intense festivity. Her outlying children had flown in the week before to celebrate her birthday a month early. The party was to be held in the new room Charlie and I were finishing in the Colonial on Wood Street. I had been in a breathless rush to complete the room before my mother's operation. And it had been well worth it. "It's so elegant!" my mother gasped (always short of breath now) when I ushered her in, the paint still drying on the walls.

At my mother's party there were gifts and cakes and poems and Champagne—alcohol connoting hope. "My doctor says I'm allowed to have one tiny sip!" my mother said in the joyous way that always seemed to come over her when her life was threatened, as it had been, her cancer returning twice. Throughout the party she floated beatifically, with the surreal peace that only seemed to come as she teetered on the verge of death. After her first breast cancer operation in 1967, she had whooped it up by taking the whole family plus cousins to the Caribbean for ten days. When she'd been diagnosed with breast cancer the third time, in 1984, she and my father had thrown a huge party at the country club on the eve of the operation, with mandatory attendance from their four adult children and their progeny. A professional photographer had been engaged at hideous expense to take a hideous photograph to be hideously framed for each member of the family—only three years hence to be tossed in attics due to sundry uncoupling.

In the middle of her last celebrate-the-tragedy party, my mother had had to rest upstairs in my bedroom. But even in this clouded moment my mother found a silver lining: lying on our king-size bed trying to catch her breath, she made the kind of momentous financial decision she tended toward on the brink of disaster. The bliss of throwing money to the winds when the bottom of life was grazed!

How well I remember the giddiness of the family in 1969 when we stayed not in one of the little-cottage motels with no TV on the highway, but a first-class hotel—after committing a brother to a mental hospital. Now, as death moved inexorably nearer, money was to be flung to the skies like confetti. After decades of sleeping in the same double bed with my father, my mother would spring for a king-size bed, and not a Simmons mattress at discount either, but a top-of-the-line Stearns & Foster—for $2,000, she didn't care. What's more, she would buy all the trappings that went with it, down to the king-size down pillows and spare set of 300-count sheets. Over we sped to Linens Plus and bang, bang, bang went my mother's charge card. What joy lay ahead, what excitement! After nearly six decades of marriage, my mother wouldn't have to lie all night on a double bed afraid her tossing and turning would wake my father. Now, in the rosy future after her operation, she would be able to worry fruitlessly all night without waking my father. The king-size bed was ordered, set to arrive when my mother was recuperating in the nursing home (it was to be a long and arduous recuperation but never mind!). "Perfect timing!" my mother exclaimed, for then it could be all set up for her when she finally arrived home. And arrive home she would, that was for sure. When my brother Johnny solemnly requested an hour alone with my mother before the operation, he was greatly pooh-poohed and made fun of and labeled a spoilsport. But Johnny, who had always understood my mother best, took the hour anyway.

Then suddenly the operation had to be put off by three days, and down from the heights my mother fell. A hopelessness grayed her face; she didn't think she could stand to wait. Now she regretted not having the operation right away as had been initially offered. She'd opted for the two extra weeks to prepare for her convalescence, when others would be privy to the unsightly corners of those living spaces that my mother (and really, most women) felt would surely condemn her in the eyes of the world. (And yet, when I'd opened my deceased mother-in-law's top drawer to find a writhing snake pit of old panty hose, I'd only liked her better for it.)

My mother had needed the extra two weeks for her youngest son, my brother Hunter, "who was so mechanical," to bustle about getting the VCR to work in the bedroom and the newly installed Call Waiting discontinued. My parents had found Call Waiting as difficult to comprehend as the ATM, whose mysteries they had vowed to unravel during a one-month vacation in Florida, only to contract the flu and abandon the project forever. My mother needed my brother Hunter to install the new phone (consisting of a large Dixieland-style Mickey Mouse playing a banjo) sent to them by faraway friends in case the faraway friends suddenly decided to turn up. Hunter, still melting hearts and as a rule so stylishly dressed (in a California way) as to be the most presentable of the four of us, managed to spend five days in and out of my parents' elegant retirement complex in a clean T-shirt and the same awful pair of scant brown-and-black ribbed shorts (it turned out he had been bought two identical pairs by a thoughtful wife). Sauntering into the ritzy lobby where the revered receptionist, Sondra, presided, through the gas-fired, carpeted living rooms and the gaily informal café filled with my parents' friends—came my brother Hunter's long, white, handsome, hairy legs and brown-sandaled feet. Down the halls and up and down the elevator with its fun notices came the hirsute legs, crossing themselves at the knee to chat up Mrs. Foster and Mrs. Greenway over a grilled cheese and tomato. For five days, I watched my mother making a brave effort in this her last week not to say anything about Hunter's shorts. *What people wear really doesn't matter in the large scheme of things*, I could see her chanting inside her brain. My poor parents, who had wanted to parade their charming, handsome son like booty, my poor parents who cared so much about clothes! Ten years earlier, on the very morning of my father's stroke, my mother had worried about getting to the cleaners, and when I'd offered to go to my dry cleaners, had cried out, "Oh, no, not there—they don't know how to do pleats!"

My mother had wanted the extra two weeks to roll up the socks in her top drawers, and categorize her closets, and knife out the hardened sticky glob way back under a kitchen drawer, and get the winter coats to storage, and have one tooth root-canaled and another capped. She needed the time to give a bureau away to my brother Johnny—father of several sons—to make room for the new zillion-dollar mattress and time to give me (four months early) the silver in one of its drawers for my twenty-fifth wedding anniversary. "Here," my mother said, yanking open a drawer of clanging metal, "take all this—I was going to give it to you anyway." And so I had held open a pillowcase while my mother plunked in two-fisted clumps of mismatched silver: old carving knives stabbing through the bottom of the pillowcase, salad forks, fish forks, fingerbowls, ornate tea-strainer spoons, butter-ball-lifter forks, and other oddly fashioned implements for outmoded dining practices—a Santa bag of treasures pouring upon me like unqualified love. For, as I was beginning to realize, I had always possessed what I had so desperately been seeking. I had only to look around my parents' apartment and see all the pictures of my mother and me, arms entwined, to understand, a little late in the game, that my mother had loved me as I had loved her, that she had been as afraid of my disapproval as I had been of hers.

Then, two days before her operation and a week ahead of schedule, the king-size bed arrived, and with a great flurry was set up, bedecked with crisp sheets and gathered bedskirt and linen bedspread and lacy throw pillows like a giant bassinet. My mother called the next day to announce that she and my father had had a great sleep in the new bed! But the following morning came the accusatory report that my mother and my father had lain awake all of their second night in the bed, as if it were the bed's fault, and not the fact that the next day my mother might die.

There is a terrible excitement that fills the New Englander at the prospect of anyone's death, even one's own—discussing my will, I always feel a tingle of excitement running down my spine. Just as catastrophe makes us cozy, so does death warm up our insides like a crackling fire. Perhaps it is because we are so rigid with our routines, and whatever death brings, it will at least be a change. Possibly it is the relief of the punishment we have so long been awaiting finally befalling us; or the belief that death will resolve at last the tangled web of our conflicting emotions. Or maybe it is as simple and as crass as the hope of a bequest. For only at death does money begin its dribble downward in the old Yankee families. "I don't want anyone to love me for my money," say the well-to-do (though not necessarily well-heeled) WASPs, and thus while they live, they are resented for their penury. But when they die! Delayed love pours out from the hearts of their heirs, themselves now too old perhaps to do much with the money but keep it from their own heirs.

And so my mother was exhilarated by the prospect of her own death. For of course, in the hidden depths of her expiring heart, she knew (and we knew) she might die. This is why in her last two months I would get frantic phone calls that she had just finished a mystery paperback and didn't have another! And why I would drop everything to rush her one, rush her anything, to numb her brain.

The operation and the aftermath, we had been warned, would be long and painful. They were, after all, breaking open my mother's eighty-three-year-old chest. They would be repairing three valves, and this would be followed by months at a rehabilitation facility. And yet, when my brothers and father and I arrived at the hospital that morning, carrying Trivial Pursuit and Scrabble and bottles of Poland Spring, the mood was heady with excitement. My mother sat up in bed to welcome us, her beautiful face alight with a transcendent glow, with no thoughts of last kisses or parting words to the family that surrounded her. For nothing is more beloved by the Protestant God than a cheerful, joking demeanor in the midst of tragedy. And so we made cracks as we followed my mother on the gurney and heard her flirtatiously asking the doctor if she could please, please keep on her wedding ring—this would be its first time off in fifty-eight years, who knew what might happen!

We had barely settled into the waiting room before the doctors came streaming in to tell us my mother was dying. The surgeon complained that he was being pressured to operate when there was a 90 percent chance she wouldn't make it if he did. I guess he wanted our permission not to operate, which, reflexively polite, we found ourselves giving. *Why not try, anyway?* we might have suddenly reconsidered. But already another doctor was informing us that my mother had died before she even got to the OR. They'd opened her up in a routine pre-op procedure and her poor clogged-up heart had never had a chance. "I guess I'm a hypochondriac," my mother had apologized a few months earlier before dragging herself to the doctor. Her diagnosis had proved she was not. She was a lady and would die in the saddle. "Whatever happens, I'm happy," she'd confided the day before the operation.

CHAPTER TWENTY-SIX

MY FATHER

AFTER MY MOTHER'S DEATH began my ten-month honey-moon with my father. I say honeymoon because all the problems that had ever plagued my parents and me dropped away, ashes to the touch, after my mother died.

Now there were no more headaches or mixed feelings, no more anger or annoyance. I wondered what had I ever been so worked up about. I could read it in my journal, but I could no longer grasp it. Instead, as I walked through town with my father, I felt weepily euphoric. All the faults I

Up past bedtime at my parents' jazz party on Main Street.

had attributed to him in the last decade were gone. He was no longer selfish or forgetful or snobbish; he was the same father I had vowed to die for when I was a teen, the sweet whistling man with the Baby Ruth candy bars in his glove compartment, who thought, despite all my efforts to prove him wrong, that I was perfect. It was as if we had already died and were angels hovering above the pettiness of human failings. None of this was fair—my mother had suffered far more on my behalf, had loved me more deeply, and had done more for all of us than my father had been capable of. When, the month after my mother's death, a brother suddenly broke up with a second wife we all adored, my father said, "Well, what can I do?" and stirred his gin and tonic. My mother would have worried all the days and nights. And yet, the truth was, when she died, I was released. Bereft, but also free. All my life I had worried she would leave me, and now that she had, the anxiety was over. Suddenly it didn't matter what anyone else thought— I was perfect the way I was.

And so, on the poignantly blue-skied afternoons of fall, my father and I would do errands together, I cherishing each second, as if I were Thoreau holding the twig of a rare something-or-other plant in his palm. Everything made us laugh and everything made us cry—a kind of heaven state. When a slight altercation arose among the brothers and me

regarding my mother's memorial service, my father sighed
and said, "Well, we'll all live—except for Jackie (my mother's nickname)." Then there was the enigma of my mother's
$2,000 dress: First of all, since when would my frugal par-
ents spend $2,000 on a dress, or had my father remembered
the price incorrectly? The dress was a long, formal silver-
gray knit which would have fallen beautifully over my
mother's elegant eighty-year-old body, had she ever worn it.
For two years it had been altered and re-altered to fit my
mother exactly right around her mastectomied chest, but
my mother, generally so easy to please, had never been
pleased. The question now was: Who owned the dress—
i.e., had my parents ever paid for it or had the extremely
polite, extremely expensive store in town that had sold my
mother the dress been waiting for her to be content with
the alterations? And if my father did own the dress, could
he possibly sell it back, now that it had been altered? When
we finally summoned our courage to visit the lovely shop
the gently born saleswomen wept at the sight of us (and we
at the sight of them), bursting out, "It's all right, Mr. Payne,
just keep the dress!" Which was so very nice (though slightly
less nice if we already owned the dress, which apparently
we would never know), and yet who wanted the dress?
Twelve years have passed and it still hangs in my closet, waiting for me to grow three inches taller and lose a breast.

THE SUNDAY BEFORE HE DIED, my father celebrated his ninety-second birthday at my house. When he woke up the next day not feeling too well, he decided to make some tapes of his banjo playing for his grandsons. When that didn't cheer him up, he wandered over to Emerson Hospital, next door.

My first thought when I arrived to find him smiling ruefully in his johnny was that maybe he had been partying too much. When the doctor in the ER asked him if he'd happened to have any alcohol the night before, my father had demurred: "Oh, no, just a couple of rum drinks and maybe two or three glasses of Champagne."

It turned out my father was bleeding to death from a benign tumor. ("Doesn't sound so benign to me," a friend said after his death.) The bleeding tumor was very large, surrounding the liver and pancreas, and could only be removed by a complicated operation in Boston. My father shook his head and said he didn't want to go through it. And so began the three heart-sinking days of trying to stop the bleeding. After everything failed, my brothers and I were told that my father couldn't be kept alive more than another twenty-four to forty-eight hours, and that it made sense, for the sake of his comfort, to stop the blood transfusions soon.

My father was not a New Englander, and for him there was no upside to his death, no cessation of suffering, just an end to his world, and to mine. So when I put the picture of my mother before him in the hospital on the theory it would give him hope for an afterlife reunion, he had pushed it away. He had adored my mother beyond all things, but now he had to keep his focus on living. "I don't want to close my eyes because I'm afraid I won't open them up again," he said. For three days my father hadn't been allowed to eat or drink anything because of tests. Still, when ginger ale and peanut butter crackers suddenly arrived, instead of being suspicious that the jig was up, my father opted for a cheerful disregard of the facts. He knew the bleeding hadn't stopped, and that his daughter couldn't stop crying, but he had never seen much point in looking too closely into things. The grandchildren were ushered in, and Popsicles passed around. I produced a bottle of Champagne, which even the youngest grandchildren were to be given. After offering the women in the room a glass first, my father lifted his glass to toast his progeny. After a while, the morphine had its effect. "Sally, maybe I'm meant to die," my father said quizzically. When I asked him if there was anything I could do for him, he said, "I'd like another glass of Champagne." Five minutes later he said, "All right, the party's over."

Later, as my father held on in a coma, the doctor told me to tell him it was okay to die. But it was not okay.

I HAD FOUGHT my parents and who they wanted me to be, at the same time wanting them to join my team. But the fact was, we had always been on the same team. And now what does it matter that the table is beautifully set for twenty at Christmas with chocolate Santas at every place, for there is no one left to approve or disapprove.

CHAPTER TWENTY-SEVEN

FLEEING MARMEE II

SEVERAL YEARS AGO, I read in *The Concord Journal* that the decrepit remains of Sophia Hawthorne and her eldest daughter were to be dug up and carted over from England to be reinterred in Concord's Sleepy Hollow. Apparently the graves were in disrepair and whoever was in charge of them had been eager to get them off his hands.

Sophia had left Concord not long after her husband's death. It probably hadn't been too hard to leave. The return to Concord in 1860, which the Hawthornes had so

---

My childhood home, on the market as I leave town.

longed for, had been a bitter disappointment. The town looked drab and provincial after a summer in Italy, and the Hawthornes had to endure not just the Alcotts next door, but the chill of abolitionist Concord's disapproval—Hawthorne having refused to renounce his old friend and college roommate, the pro-slavery president, Franklin Pierce. Back in Concord, despite building a splendid writing tower onto his house, Hawthorne found he couldn't write well; four years later he was dead.

Tour guides in Concord claim Hawthorne for our own. Yet when the coffins of Sophia and her daughter were paraded through town by horse-drawn carriage, I knew of no one who attended the procession or was even aware it was happening. I suppose this is because we all know, deep down, that Hawthorne does not really belong to Concord. When Hawthorne wrote about his "strange, indolent, unjoyous attachment for my native town," it was not Concord he was referring to, but Salem, the town where he had been a child, if not a happy child. Hawthorne was over forty when, impoverished, he had regretfully left The Old Manse for his mother's house in Salem. And it was back in Salem that he had written his most famous book. Still, whenever I read the passage in Hawthorne's preface to *The Scarlet Letter* about returning to his hometown, I am moved—and I wish that Hawthorne had lived longer and written more:

Soon, likewise, my old native town will loom upon
me through the haze of memory, . . . as if it were no
portion of the real earth . . . Henceforth it ceases
to be a reality of my life; I am a citizen of somewhere else. My good townspeople will not much regret me, for—though it has been as dear an object
as any, in my literary efforts, to be of some importance in their eyes and to win myself a pleasant
memory in this abode and burial-place of so many
of my forefathers—there has never been, for me, the
genial atmosphere which a literary man requires . . .
I shall do better amongst other faces; and these familiar ones, it need hardly be said, will do just as
well without me.

"I FEEL GUILTY ALL THE TIME, I don't know why," says
Hunter at age twenty-one.

Graduating from college, no one can get out of Concord faster than Teddy or Hunter, bridling at the privileged
world which once gave them so much joy. No one is more
eager to get away from the woodland trails and glittering
ponds and buzzing fields of wildflowers, from the playing
fields where a thousand years ago on freezing spring evenings they'd pitched and whacked the ball far into the

sunset, as if childhood would never end. No one is more ready to trade in unlocked front doors and heartbreakingly cozy houses for cramped, beat-up apartments in the city with hefty security deposits and car-towing fines. But what Hunter and Teddy cannot know is that though they leave this town, it will never leave them. Somewhere in their souls will lurk the impossible premise that a Concord youth imparts: that all will be happy in the end.

And in my heart today, I struggle to believe that happy lie from my Protestant youth. For I too am leaving Concord at last—moving out of New England to New York, away, away, finally away—after living here in limbo these past four years waiting for Emily to graduate from high school. Emily does not long to get away; it is over her I beat my retreat, trampling over the idyll of her entire life to date. Emily is nostalgic over her childhood while it is still in progress, missing Concord even while we linger here—like Thoreau, languishing for months in his mother's house. She misses best-friends-turned-enemies, certain trees, lemonade stands, the dirt sidewalk beneath her feet, and the iced-over puddle in front of Sally Ann's through which her party shoe once so tragically plunged. A freshman in high school, she returns home from volleyball camp to breathe in wonder, "The kids from New Jersey have never even *heard* of Concord." And how could she not have been surprised when every year of her life has been cocooned in Concord historicity, from field trips to the Concord museum to church invitations to retrace the (not very happy, but never mind) trip Emerson had taken to Rome in 1832. The world has gotten over Concord, but we who grow up here cannot.

AND SO, fifty years after my family first came to Concord, I sell my last Concord house. As God and everyone else knows, it is time for me to leave my hometown, time to leave my childhood and my children's childhood too. Time to go, to leave behind the matrons of my youth before they leave me first—for the great pasture (under conservation) in the sky—to become without them who I really am. And so I pay my last fine at the public library; go to my last back-to-school night at the high school, where so long ago I'd roamed the halls in ironed hair and Indian print miniskirt and hoped Toby Raker would deign to say hello. I allow Miss Flora from my first grade to rest in peace and Ms. Groe from Teddy and Hunter's too. I say good-bye to the Alcott School and the Thoreau School and the former Peter Bulkeley School (now low-income housing for the elderly) and drink the last draught of Emerson Playground din. I release at last, though not without another embarrassing wrench, Nashawtuc Hill and the view of the river's turn, and all my hopes and pretensions of being rich, or accepted, or even safe. I bid good-bye to the second half of my children's childhood. Good-bye to Hunter at fifteen, who (as I was informed by his conscientious brother) refused to watch *Seinfeld* with the family because he hated to hear me laugh; to Hunter at seventeen, quoting poetry as with tattooed arm he chugged from the milk carton; to Hunter at eighteen, suddenly back in my life again, wanting to chat so often that I had to schedule in an extra hour in my day— only to leave for college. Good-bye to Teddy at fifteen, the cartoon thought-bubble appearing over his head—*What kind of moron is this?*—every time I ask his help to turn on the TV; to Teddy at sixteen, disqualified from playing in Battle of the Bands because his band doesn't have a singer, and me up all night every night chanting hopelessly to myself, *Teddy doesn't have a singer for his band*, until the sad night arrived, and suddenly there was Teddy packing up his car with amps and I daring to ask, and Teddy shrugging, "Oh, we got a singer two weeks ago," and departing to win second prize.

Good-bye to the Ladies Four O'Clock Club, whose members, rendered innocuous at last, even cute, I weep to leave. Good-bye to all the mothers my age I was so afraid of when I became a mother, but who turned out to be afraid of me. Good-bye to "Thing," Hunter's first girlfriend, and all my children's friends and enemies; good-bye to the Different Drummer restaurant, and good-bye to Sutton and Murphy, our premarital dogs who journeyed with us to Watertown, New Hampshire, Boston, New York City, Dobbs Ferry, Cambridge, finally to end their days in Concord. Good-bye to Mrs. Potter, whose family life had always seemed so impossibly perfect, but who has unhappily outlived a child and husband. Good-bye to Twinky Warren, and Jib, and Jab, and all the rest, who, I dearly hope, will walk their dogs and run this town and pay their $5 annual dues into eternity, enjoying the certainty of who they are and where they are—just as they did, and will do, without me forever more.

Good-bye to Emerson, whose sunlit library I wish were mine. Good-bye to all my struggles against Thoreau, whose writing, after all of it, I will probably be clasping as I die. Good-bye to Louisa May Alcott, the architect of happy daughterhood, whose warming depictions of the life she wished she'd had strike me deeper today knowing she never had it. Good-bye to *Little Women* and all the Concord Players performances of *Little Women*—from my sacred first to my sacred last, which I had attended with full heart shortly before we left town, settling in on a folding wooden seat on the rippling floor of the creaky old theater on Walden Street to inhale the nostalgia I'd become addicted to. And then, as had so often happened these past two decades, while I was thinking about my past, a part of my past appeared—Mrs. Coyle, my parents' friend and once a member of the Main Street crowd, though even in the 1960s different from the rest, less bound by Concord mores, more cosmopolitan. Mrs. Coyle, who had played Amy so many years ago in the Concord Players production in which my mother's friends, each a mother several times over, had valiantly played the teenage girls. "I killed your father!" the still-beautiful octogenarian Mrs. Coyle cries out only half facetiously as she rushes up to me—because, she tells me, he had insisted upon carrying her very heavy suitcase all the way down Walden Street to Weezie Winthrop's funeral service. "Of course you didn't kill my father," I assure her profusely. But later I think that even if lugging the heavy suitcase had precipitously begun the bleeding that sent my ninety-two-year-old father to the hospital two days later, how honored he would have been to die of gallantry, especially to the charming Mrs. Coyle, so "wellborn" and yet so un-Concord glamorous.

Good-bye to all the Concord houses I have loved. Good-bye to the dark, low-ceilinged abodes of Louisa Alcott's impoverished childhood, where Marmee's bad teeth prevented her eating the apples that were Bronson's imposed staple. Good-bye to lofty Orchard House, where I (and millions of others) had imagined the real Little Women had lived—but where, in fact, the women were no longer little—Beth six feet under by then, Anna engaged, and Louisa old at thirty. Good-bye to the yellow house on Main Street, where the dying Thoreau had asked that his attic bed be dragged into his mother's parlor where he wouldn't miss anything. And good-bye to the rather Ralph Laurenish replica of Thoreau's cabin where Thoreau had lived so economically, on Emerson's land.

Good-bye to The Old Manse, where a young Emerson wrote "Nature" on a visit and a middle-aged Hawthorne found happiness in marriage. Good-bye to Emerson's grand white house at the mouth of town—where Margaret Fuller had dismounted from the stagecoach to rattle Mrs. Emerson's nerves. Good-bye to The Wayside (the former Hillside), the only house Hawthorne ever owned, though not for long.

And good-bye to the houses where my children played: to the giant, wondrous houses of their earliest friends; to the house on Nashawtuc Hill, sold recently for four times what we paid for it and doubled in size; to our last house, whose interior I had so improved that my parents had finally said, "We like this house more than the house on Nashawtuc Hill," warming my shallow soul. Good-bye to the glorious assisted-living facility where my parents' best friends have moved at last. Good-bye to my parents, now buried in Sleepy Hollow. And good-bye to my own child-hood home on Main Street—which happened to be on the market as we left town, and where I stopped to take a quick look, resisting mightily the temptation to make an offer.

I was first enthralled with the terrible Bronson Alcott—the "majestic egotist"—while reading Odell Shepard's amazing 1937 biography: *Pedlar's Progress: The Life of Bronson Alcott* (I later turned to Shepard's edition of *The Journals of Bronson Alcott* as reference). Nowhere near as good, but interesting because it was written by two who knew him, is *A. Bronson Alcott: His Life and Philosophy,* by F. B. Sanborn and William T. Harris. Thoreau was pretty funny about Bronson (he once described Bronson as *nowhere doing nothing*), but Louisa was funnier (see *Bronson Alcott's Fruitlands with Transcendental Wild Oats,* by Clara Endicott Sears and Louisa May Alcott). Sad and revealing were *The Journals of Louisa May Alcott*, edited by Joel Myerson and Daniel Shealy, as well as *Louisa May Alcott: Her Life, Letters and Journals,* edited by Ednah D. Cheney. Bronson had an ill-disguised, middle-aged crush on Cheney when she was young and not yet Mrs. Cheney, which his daughters seemed to know about. Later she got monstrously fat, as described by Anna Alcott. Also essential to my understanding were the wonderful *Louisa May Alcott: A Modern Biography,* by Martha Saxton; *Louisa May Alcott: A Biography,* by Madeleine B. Stern; *The Alcotts: Biography of a Family,* by Madelon Bedell; and *Marmee and Louisa: The Untold Story of Louisa May Alcott and Her Mother,* by Eve LaPlante. LaPlante also wrote a fascinating book about Anne Hutchinson (*American Jezebel: The Uncommon Life of Anne Hutchinson, the Woman Who Defied the Puritans*). Speaking of the Puritans, the best book I read about them in a modern way is a novel by a Spaniard who didn't come to this country until his teens—*The Last Puritan,* by George Santayana. (For old-fashioned Puritans, read Perry Miller's *Errand into the Wilderness.*) *May Alcott: A Memoir,* by Caroline Ticknor, was deeply revealing about May ("Amy"), who *was* kind of icky but also brave.

Anyone who reads Thoreau in editions annotated by the great Jeffrey S. Cramer (especially *Walden: A Fully Annotated Edition* and *I to Myself: An Annotated Selection from the Journals of Henry D. Thoreau*) will know everything there is to know about Thoreau and (amazingly) have a fun time learning it. For pure humor (but not necessarily total accuracy), read *Thoreau, The Poet-Naturalist,* by William E. Channing, the slacker poet who professed to be Thoreau's great friend and then threw him under the wagon (saying, for instance, that Thoreau didn't live at Walden—he "bivouacked there and really lived at home. . . ."). Hilarious too, but in a smart way, is Perry Miller's *Consciousness in Concord: The Text of Thoreau's Hitherto Lost Journal (1840–1841),* together with notes and a commentary, about Thoreau's supposedly heartbreaking romance with his brother's fiancée. Sweet and moving is *Henry Thoreau As Remembered by a Young Friend,* by Edward Emerson, which begins with Emerson's son defending Thoreau against his townsmen, who consider him an arrogant, lazy woods-burner. Other great books about Thoreau: *Henry Thoreau: A Life of the Mind,* by Robert D. Richardson, Jr.; *The Days of Henry Thoreau: A Biography,* by Walter Harding; *Concord's Happy Rebel,* by Hildegarde Hawthorne; and *Young Man Thoreau,* by Richard Lebeaux.

After I read the following—*The Essential Writings of Ralph Waldo Emerson,* edited by Brooks Atkinson; *Emerson Among the Eccentrics: A Group Portrait,* by Carlos Baker; *Emerson: The Roots of Prophecy,* by Evelyn Barrish; *Emerson: The Mind on Fire,* by Robert D. Richardson, Jr.; and *The Life of Ralph Waldo Emerson,* by Ralph L. Rusk—I was ready to marry Emerson, without ever having heard his mellifluous voice. Apparently, girls swooned when he spoke. He was dangerously flirtatious early in his marriage to Lidian, exchanging love notes in his house with the reckless Margaret Fuller, but after his young son died, he changed and the marriage to Lidian was secured. Still, it is hard not to feel sympathy for the somber woman who had begun marriage as second fiddle to a romantically dead first wife. I loved both *Mr. Emerson's Wife,* a novel by Amy Belding Brown, and *The Life of Lidian Jackson Emerson,* by Ellen Tucker Emerson, edited by Delores Bird Carpenter.

A twentysomething Henry James lectured a good-natured Louisa May Alcott (ten years his senior) at a dinner party, but he never knew the much older (and at that point, dead) Hawthorne. Nevertheless, in his midthirties, he wrote a brilliant book (*Hawthorne*), admiring the author's "delicate talent," but less so the New England that "seems to blow through his pages." James admitted later that he hadn't been able to refrain from overusing the word "provincial" in his description of Concord and the region. I must also mention somewhere Megan Marshall's illuminating book about the Peabody sisters (of whom Sophia Hawthorne was one, and Bronson's partner in his disastrous Boston school, Elizabeth, another), which featured some not-to-be-forgotten scenes with an hysterical Marmee defending her husband (*The Peabody Sisters: Three Women*

Who Ignited American Romanticism). Also deeply interesting were *Mosses from an Old Manse* and *The Scarlet Letter,* by Hawthorne; *Hawthorne in Concord,* by Philip McFarland; and *Hawthorne: A Life,* by Brenda Wineapple.

Emerson had the galley before him of *A History of the Town of Concord (1835)* by Lemuel Shattuck when he spoke at Concord's bicentennial celebration, and he took his startled townsmen to task for sins committed against the Concord Indians some 150 years earlier. The stuff about the first Puritans trying to be fair to Indians was so funny in Shattuck's book I wrote two chapters on the subject, which readers have been spared. Other books about Concord (mostly by Concordians) I found fascinating were *The People of Concord: One Year in the Flowering of New England,* by Paul Brooks; *Concord: Then & Now,* by Sarah Chapin, Claiborne Dawes and Alice Moulton; *Concord: Stories to Be Told, A Massachusetts Town Memoir,* by Liz Nelson; *Memorabilia of Hawthorne Alcott and Concord,* by Franklin Benjamin Sanborn, edited by Kenneth Walter Cameron; *Nay-Saying in Concord: Emerson, Alcott, and Thoreau,* by Stoehr Taylor; *Classic Concord,* by Caroline Ticknor; and *Concord: Climate for Freedom,* by Ruth R. Wheeler.

ACKNOWLEDGMENTS

First, I would like to thank the great Sandy Frazier.

Also: Priscilla Warner, for rescuing this book in its darkest hours;

Jeannie Jordan, for mercifully deleting chapters that will never be missed;

Charlie Stuart, heroic reader of a thousand terrible drafts;

Steven Erat, for his exquisite, evocative photos;

Sarah Stein, for pulling it all together;

Liz Darhansoff, for never despairing;

And Sarah McGrath, who made this book a dream come true.

PHOTOGRAPHY CREDITS